T0154752

REPORTING FOR ARKANSAS

THE ARKANSAS CHARACTER

Robert Cochran, Series Editor

REPORTING FOR ARKANSAS

The Documentary Films of Jack Hill

DALE CARPENTER and ROBERT COCHRAN

The University of Arkansas Press
Fayetteville
2022

ISBN: 978-1-68226-207-8
eISBN: 978-1-61075-776-8

26 25 24 23 22   5 4 3 2 1

Manufactured in the United States of America

Designed by Liz Lester

∞ The paper used in this publication meets the minimum requirements of the American National Standard for Permanence of Paper for Printed Library Materials Z39.48-1984.

Library of Congress Cataloging-in-Publication Data

Names: Carpenter, Dale (Documentary filmmaker), author. |
    Cochran, Robert, 1943– author.
Title: Reporting for Arkansas: the documentary films of Jack Hill /
    Dale Carpenter and Robert Cochran.
Description: Fayetteville: The University of Arkansas Press, 2022. |
    Series: Arkansas character series | Includes bibliographical ref-
    erences and index. | Summary: "In Reporting for Arkansas, Dale
    Carpenter and Robert Cochran present a biography of the pio-
    neering Arkansas documentarian Jack Hill alongside a filmogra-
    phy celebrating the reissue of several of Hill's works newly hosted
    online by the David and Barbara Pryor Center for Arkansas Oral
    and Visual History"—Provided by publisher.
Identifiers: LCCN 2021050726 (print) | LCCN 2021050727 (ebook) |
    ISBN 9781682262078 (paperback) | ISBN 9781610757768 (ebook)
Subjects: LCSH: Hill, Jack E. (Jack Edward), 1940–2012. |
    Motion picture producers and directors—Arkansas—
    Biography. | Television journalists—Arkansas—Biography. |
    Documentary films—Production and direction—Arkansas. |
    Arkansas—Biography.
Classification: LCC PN1998.3.H536 C37 2022 (print) | LCC
    PN1998.3.H536 (ebook) | DDC 070.1/8092—dc23/eng/20211120
LC record available at https://lccn.loc.gov/2021050726
LC ebook record available at https://lccn.loc.gov/2021050727

For Anne Hill

CONTENTS

Bonus Tracks

SERIES EDITOR'S PREFACE

Reporting for Arkansas had its origins in a 2014–15 museum exhibit at the Old State House Museum in Little Rock celebrating the state's role in Hollywood films. Working on a "Bonus Feature" chapter on documentary films for the exhibit catalog, *Lights! Camera! Arkansas!*, Suzanne McCray and I kept hearing stories about Jack Hill. Twenty-five years earlier he had created in Little Rock an independent video production company, TeleVision for Arkansas, and over a two-decade period produced close to seventy films. Our most fruitful initial inquiries took place at the University of Arkansas in Fayetteville, where Dale Carpenter and Larry Foley, journalism professors and documentary filmmakers, filled us in on Hill's career. Carpenter had been a cameraman, often the only cameraman, for at least half of Hill's films.

The immediate result was a paragraph-length thumbnail bio/filmography in the exhibit's catalog, but by that time it was clear Hill's work deserved fuller treatment. *Reporting for Arkansas* really got its start a year later when Carpenter first loaned his VHS copies of Hill's films and then agreed to collaborate in a sustained attempt at retrieval and redistribution of Hill's best work. Six years later, delayed but not derailed by the COVID-19 pandemic, it arrives as the fourth volume in the Arkansas Character series cosponsored by Fulbright College's Center for Arkansas and Regional Studies and the David and Barbara Pryor Center for Arkansas Oral and Visual History. *Reporting for Arkansas* features an online video component, a first for the series, produced by Pryor Center staff, who designed it to match the book's format. Hill had two decades as an award-winning television journalist under his belt when, exiled from a cherished profession, he turned in midlife to documentary film, where he soon learned to make beautifully executed oral history interviews core highlights of his productions. *Reporting for Arkansas*, with more than eight hours of his most accomplished work, is thus itself a substantial compilation of Arkansas oral and visual history.

Books are appreciated by those who love them as harmonious confluences of intellect, artistry, and craftsmanship. Authors get their names on fronts and spines, but they ride the shoulders not only of others who help them get the book written but also of others who take their sheaf of paper (or its electronic equivalent) and bring editorial and artistic skills to myriad selections of type fonts and sizes, paper weights and finishes and the like, to design, format, print, bind, and deliver to readers a handsome volume. *Reporting for Arkansas*, given its central video component, was brought to completion by a larger-than-usual cohort of helping hands. Thanks are owed to many.

Anne Hill, Jack's widow, comes first in this group. Introduced to the nascent project in a 2016 Little Rock interview, she offered constant encouragement and repeatedly helped in contacting friends and colleagues all over the state and nation. Cassandra Greene, at the Rogers High School library, dug up and cheerfully loaned Mountie yearbooks from 1957 and 1958. A copy of Hill's MA thesis, "A Survey of Network Television's Coverage of the War in Vietnam," was provided by Gary Cox, reference archivist at the University of Missouri Library.

Cecilia Tisdale at the Mississippi Department of Archives and History in Jackson helped secure a copy of *Homes like These*, Hill's first award-winning film. Telephone interviews with Carroll and Sally Fulgham provided background on Hill's time at Jackson's WLBT television station.

Hill's decade-long Jonesboro stint at KAIT was recalled by Becky Allison and Ray Scales in a lengthy interview session at Pastor Scales's Jonesboro church in July 2018 and by Darrel Cunningham in an October 2018 interview in Fort Smith. Interviews in Rogers with high school friend Mack Luffman (in October 2018) and family friend Bonnie Grimes (in September 2019) were a great help in filling in details of Hill's early life. The terrific Fayetteville historian Charlie Allison provided a wonderful account of the University of Arkansas Press Club and various journalism honorary societies, and Shiloh Peters's searches of newspaper accounts provided important assistance in understanding Hill's role in the criminal prosecutions of Coolidge Conlee and Wayne DuMond.

If our marathon sessions viewing the entire range of Hill's sixty-five to seventy films led us to understand his 1994 *Work Will Win* as possessing pivotal significance in locating a particular topical sweet spot for his future work, it was Dr. Calvin King, president of the Arkansas Land and Community Development Corporation, who taught us most about its origins. We also received generous assistance from Director Elizabeth Harward at the Jacksonville Museum of Military History, Vice-President Albert Jones at the Arkansas Land and Community Development Corporation in Fargo, Assistant Superintendent Tim Scott at Devil's Den

State Park, and Principal Shane Storey at Charleston High School.

Initial searches for extant copies of Hill's films were aided by David Elmore at what was then the Arkansas Educational Television Network (AETN). The major archive of such copies is the Special Collections Division at the University of Arkansas Library in Fayetteville, where Amy Allen, Lori Birrell, Misha Gardner, Melody Herr, Blair Hollender, Kasey Kelm, Lora Lennertz, Deena Owens, Geoffery Stark, Katrina Windon, and Joshua Youngblood provided unstinting aid through the rigors of the COVID-19 pandemic. At the Pryor Center, Randy Dixon and Scott Lunsford scanned various now-obsolete formats to obtain usable copies of several films, and the entire video playlist accompanying this volume was designed, edited, and uploaded by Susan Kendrick-Perry, Steff Leffler, and Sarah Moore. At the University of Arkansas Press, the Carpenter/Cochran "sheaf of paper" was taken competently in hand by Mike Bieker, David Scott Cunningham, Janet Foxman, Katie Herman, Melissa King, Liz Lester, and Charlie Shields. Finishing touches to the manuscript were supplied by photographers Sabine Schmidt and Don House, authors of *Remote Access: Small Public Libraries in Arkansas*, volume three in the Arkansas Character series, who undertook a two-day journey in May of 2021, gathering contemporary images from sites where Hill made his most memorable films.

When Jack Hill died in 2012, his widow, Anne, awarded broadcast rights to his films to AETN, now Arkansas PBS. We are grateful to Executive Director and CEO Courtney Pledger for permission to upload our chosen selections from Hill's work and for spearheading a round of new programming in support of this volume's release.

Reporting for Arkansas marks a new level in the synergistic meshing of the Center for Arkansas and Regional Studies with the David and Barbara Pryor Center for Arkansas Oral and Visual History. Bill and Judy Schwab, then dean of Fulbright College and associate vice-chancellor of the University of Arkansas, respectively, originated the linkage. Bill now directs the Pryor Center. His leadership, along with strong support and direction from current Fulbright dean Todd Shields, has made possible higher levels of performance for both programs. The four volumes of the Arkansas Character series, and especially this one, are tangible instances.

If first thanks went to Anne Hill for her initial encouragement understood as authorization, final thanks is due to Dale Carpenter for agreeing to co-author this volume. I never met Jack Hill and have little experience and no training as a filmmaker or film historian. Without the guarantee of Carpenter's knowing counsel and collaboration, this volume would not have been undertaken.

ROBERT COCHRAN

STRAIGHT ARROW

Jack Edward Hill was from start to finish a serious person, the only child of a war-hero father and a revered schoolteacher mother, raised from birth to mainstream ideals of service and excellence. Born in 1940, he wastes no time doing such parents proud. As a youth he wears many uniforms. In high school, he's president of his class, makes the National Honor Society, plays on a state championship basketball team, and graduates with most-likely-to-succeed laurels in 1958. He stars in a local-hero-saves-child newspaper story for rescuing a child as a pool lifeguard the summer after his junior year at the University of Arkansas, where he serves as chaplain at his fraternity house and is initiated into the military student honor society in the ROTC program before graduating in 1962 with a BA in speech.

For the next two years, he serves in Cold War Germany as a lieutenant in the US Army. Honorably discharged, he earns a master's degree in journalism at the University of Missouri and launches his career as a broadcast journalist with brief stints in Colorado (Denver), Mississippi (Jackson), and Texas (Dallas) before coming back to Arkansas as news anchor at KAIT in Jonesboro. The year is 1975, he's newly married, and he's ready to make a name.

This doesn't take long. Hill becomes something of a star, an on-camera anchor with the dogged tenacity and fearlessness of an investigative reporter. Working with ace cameraman Ray Scales, the station's first African American employee, Hill produces pieces on slum housing, railroad crossing safety, corruption in the St. Francis County Sheriff's Office, and white supremacist survivalists that win national-level awards from associations of his peers. It is a glorious time—and people remember it. (When Hill dies in 2012, memorial notices call him "Arkansas' best and perhaps most prolific broadcast journalist" and refer to him as a "local news legend."[1])

But then, a decade in, it all ends, suddenly and ingloriously. On July 23, 1985, the big winner suddenly finds himself out of a job, axed not for insufficient but for excessive devotion to journalistic standards. He's forty-five years old. For a decade he's worked for the largest station in a sprawling, mostly rural region's largest town. He's a company man, accustomed to working with supportive colleagues on a journalistic team. He loves the excitement of breaking news, the adventure of pursuing the day's top stories. Journalism, the vital First Amendment role of a free press, is a perfect occupation for the job he understands himself as born to, a natural expression of the service credo imbibed from birth. He's proud of the work, the progress ideal it serves, his respected position in the community. Just two years before, he flew to New York to accept a national award from Columbia University's top-notch journalism school, with star PBS anchor Robert "Robin" MacNeil presenting the plaque. His boss at KAIT, the man who hired him, would call this moment a high point of *his* career. But now he's out, a victim of corporate restructurings coupled with absence of managerial backbone. It's a sudden-onset midlife crisis on steroids.

Hill takes five years to find his footing, but once he does the day of disaster is recognized as opportunity's hard knock. He will move from crackerjack employee to successful entrepreneur, end up topping his decade as an ace broadcast journalist with more than twice that time as a pioneer of longform documentary filmmaking in Arkansas. Over a twenty-three-year period, working as a one-man operation, developing projects, writing grants and scripts, hiring camera operators, and selling sponsorships, he produces and directs nearly seventy titles and arranges for their broadcast on a wide range of commercial stations across Arkansas (plus one in Monroe, Louisiana) and the Arkansas Educational Television Network (AETN). As he works, he develops a standard structural format: An opening teaser is followed by an on-camera stand-up. "I'm Jack Hill," the producer says as he introduces the film's subject. His appearances thereafter are brief, the now-seated interviewer listening intently to featured talking heads. But then, always, there's a standard close, Hill back for the sign-off. "This is Jack Hill," he says, "reporting for Arkansas." This handed us our title.

We have prepared this account in a single authorial voice, combining the extensive experience with Hill and his films of one author with the archival and biographical research of the other. Our undertaking is rooted in a shared sense of the appeal of Hill's work as documentary cinema that gains value over time from the double focus characteristic of his approach from the beginning. Hill's best productions, that is, are never composed wholly or even primarily of archival footage. His signature move seeks out and interviews people for whom the past events they recall are vivid memories retaining substantial present-day appeal. The saga of Union County's oil boom, the tale of Arkansas's World War II POW camps, the beautifully told story of the Arkansas Ordnance Plant in Jacksonville, the account of the vital role played by Civilian Conservation Corps camps in the lives of young men and their families in Depression-era Arkansas—these and many other Hill productions thus offer a view not only into the time and place of their subjects, but also into the less remote milieu of their making.

Our book divides neatly into two parts. We lead off with an extended biographical sketch, more substantial than a biographical dictionary entry but much shorter than a complete life history, followed by a title-by-title discussion of the films selected as representative of Hill's best work. Both sections are arranged in chronological order. That film is a perishable medium is made vividly apparent by the fact that several of Hill's productions were lost or difficult to locate when we began our work, only five years after his death, surviving thanks to the efforts of archives scattered across the state (and region in several instances). Taken as a whole, his films constitute a very rough, deeply idiosyncratic visual analogue of *Arkansas: A Narrative History*, the current standard text for passing on the state's heritage to the state's school children. The latter is a book, the combined work of four distinguished authors written as a work of traditional history, aiming at the fullest feasible record, balanced treatment, celebration muted with clear-eyed assessment. The former is a set of films, the work of a single producer-director assisted by a varying phalanx of videographers and editors, less constrained by the requirements of objective history and thus more openly celebratory in tone and aiming above all to hold the attention of viewers with remotes ready to hand.

Our point in making this comparison is to stress the overlap. Hill's best work, the films originating from his own initiative in the final third of his life, is most appropriately valued as a form of popular history. We undertook this labor of preservation and presentation out of a conviction that pieces like *Doing What Was Right*, *Dollar a Day and All You Can Eat*, and *Arkansas' Black Gold*, among many others, offer themselves as wonderful resources both for classroom use and for viewing by a wider public. That Hill designed them with pedagogical ends in view is made clear by the budget lines in his grant proposals providing for paid committees of educators to produce printed guides for teachers. At their best they are also engaging cinema—compelling visual sequences of Arkansas people busy in their lives in a wide range of Arkansas places are everywhere in them. Soft-spoken old men who were cruel-minded schoolboys in the 1920s reminisce in a Piggott café about throwing stones at the Hemingway they took for a bum. Children who recognize her car and know her schedule gather in the parking lot of an Arkadelphia apartment complex to unload meals a local woman delivers from a Little Rock food bank. A distinguished Arkansas attorney and former US senator recalls with understated pride his role in integrating Charleston schools.

Such anecdotal scenes, vivid as they are, never appear solely for their visual lyricism or aesthetic appeal, though these qualities often break through.

Rather, they invariably find their subordinate place in an overarching narrative. Hill is not a documentary filmmaker who will be remembered primarily for the specifically cinematic excellence of his work. He was first and last a photographic journalist with a story to tell. He came to film as a newsman, and if a poet (fascist dupe Ezra Pound) once described literature as "news that STAYS news,"[2] Hill eventually made his own name for news of enduring import. He called it history, and he was convinced that knowing at least some of it, the more the better, fostered a sense of community life. His opening stand-ups and closing sign-offs signal his goals with headline-size clarity. What is coming on the screen, he says, will be fact, not fiction, an episode of Arkansas life ordered into coherent narrative. He is telling it like it is, "reporting for Arkansas." If you pay attention, he promises, an enhanced sense of your home ground's saga will be nurtured. From the beginning, Hill was determined to arrange for his work to be exhibited on commercial stations. AETN, now Arkansas PBS, would prove a vital source of both exposure and financial support, the most dependable outlet for his work (and today an important archive for its preservation). But his core audience as he dreamed it was larger. "The people who watch public television already appreciate Arkansas history," he told Dale Carpenter. "I'm after Joe Six-Pack."

And Joe's family, we might add, remembering the teachers' guides and the thousands of tapes distributed to schools and libraries. What's more, there's a perceptible class component in Hill's choice of locution—Joe is a working man (or woman)—as well as an overriding geographical emphasis. Joe's whole family lives in Arkansas, and it sums up Jack Hill's career nicely to note that he devoted its final twenty plus years to telling the state's signature stories to a statewide audience. These considerations guided our selection of the films that headline this project. The archive at the University of Arkansas includes several titles from Hill's days at KAIT, and a copy of his initial long-form award winner, *Homes like These*, has been preserved in Mississippi. We screened all these—in fact we screened every Jack Hill film we could find—but our decision at the end of the day was to reissue films Hill himself might have chosen as best representing his purposes were he alive today to make the selection. His pride in what he called the "Arkansas Series" was well founded, we thought, and the accompanying playlist is for the most part fairly described as an updated version of that list. We have presented our account in a shared authorial voice throughout, though certain passages relating firsthand experience with Hill are identified as Carpenter's.

Hill labored diligently at this work until he died of cancer in 2012, busy nearly to the end with a compilation of his several Civil War documentaries into an extended portrait of Arkansas's role in the conflict. His surviving films, products of the twentieth century's final decade and the twenty-first's first, constitute at once a significant oral history record from those years and an invaluable contribution to mainstream presentation of Arkansas history. They need to not be lost. Our selection from them, as large as we could make it, is the heart of this project.

We credit Hill's sign-off as a deliberate choice—this is a man who wrote his own scripts, who learned over a long career to choose his terms carefully. He could easily have used "reporting from Arkansas," for example. But "for" was a better choice. At its most resonant, we are convinced, his phrasing succinctly communicated, every time he said it, both a semi-covert expression of mission and an explicit proffering of gift.

PART I

TO ARRIVE WHERE
HE STARTED

CHAPTER 1

SERIOUS PEOPLE

Rogers

In 2012, too sick to attend a ceremony awarding him a Lifetime Achievement Award from the Arkansas Historical Association, Jack Hill recorded a video-taped statement of appreciation for the gathered history buffs. His love of the past, he told an anticipated audience he was confident would share it, went back to his earliest memories. Born in 1940 as the only child of William Radus Hill (1911–89) and Grace Fields Hill (1915–2012) just eighteen months before Pearl Harbor catapulted the United States into what became the Second World War, Hill spent much of his early childhood living with his mother and maternal grandparents while his father served in the US Army in Europe. He thought he must have been about four when they realized that propping him up on the sofa of their Springdale, Arkansas, home with two large volumes of Civil War history would get them surprisingly extended periods of settled quiet.

He couldn't really read yet, Hill recalled, but the books featured numerous photographs, maps, and other illustrations, and the youngster reportedly spent hours paging attentively through them.

Young history buff, Rogers, Arkansas, ca. 1941. *Photograph courtesy of Anne Hill.*

His elders were greatly impressed. Once he was old enough to climb down from the sofa and join his neighborhood age-mates in childhood war games, he stood out among his rebel-sympathizer pals, according to his wife's later recollections, for his insistence on always enlisting on the Union side. Though he would grow up to pursue a career in broadcast journalism, he would throughout his life retain a more than casual interest in history in general and military history in particular. His spouse's patience would be repeatedly tested by her husband's insistence on stopping on vacations for careful examination of "every last roadside historical marker," and the sizeable collection of papers bequeathed to the University of Arkansas after his death would include boxes of saved back issues of *MHQ: The Quarterly Journal of Military History*.

The focus on journalism, especially broadcast journalism, also surfaced early. First as a high school student (with local Rogers station KAMO) and later as a college undergraduate at the University of Arkansas in Fayetteville (with KHOG), Hill would get his start as a radio broadcaster. The 1957 edition of *The Mountaineer*, the Rogers High School yearbook for his junior year, includes a shot of him at the microphone for *Mountaineer Time*, listed as a "Saturday afternoon radio program." Hill was an all-around star at Rogers High—his wide smile also shows up not only in his class picture but also in photos of him as "Student Body Vice-President," "Vice-President" of the student council, and a member of the varsity basketball team.[1] (That squad won Rogers High's only state basketball championship, though the yearbook must have gone to press too early to include the triumph.)

He's even more prominently featured in the edition from 1958, when he was a senior. The basketball team photo and the student council shot appear again, along with an individual senior portrait, but most prominent of all is the photo at the very front of the volume, where "Jack Edward Hill, President of Student Body," smiling as widely as ever and decked out in a checked sport coat and bow tie, gets second billing next to Superintendent of Schools Greer Lingle, knocking his own principal, L. N. Gaines, to the following page. Inside, there's a two-page spread where Hill is pictured three times, looking contemplative in a second student body president shot and making a first appearance as a member of the Senior High Honor Society.[2] The yearbooks include no mention of it, but according to Anne Hill's recollection, Jack was also voted "most likely to succeed" by his classmates.

The memories of one classmate, recorded sixty years after their high school graduation, accord nicely with the impression of ambition and seriousness conveyed by the yearbook record. Mack Luffman and Hill were childhood friends—their fathers both worked at the Rogers Coca-Cola plant owned by Luffman's grandfather, and "our mothers were close." Born in the same year, the boys attended school together "until Rogers built its second elementary school and Jack E. went to the new school and I stayed behind at the old one," Luffman recalled. "We were back together all through junior high and high school." Cautioning his listener not to make too much of it, Luffman referred to Hill as "Jack E." throughout the interview: "We all called him 'Jack E.' It wasn't 'Jackie.' His mother called him 'Jack E.' That was his name, as far as everyone who knew him was concerned."

Luffman's recollections repeatedly stressed the qualities of character one might expect of a student body president and honor society member: "He was extremely serious in everything that he did. He's the only person I know of, in the whole history of the Rogers Schools, who had perfect attendance—from the first day of first grade until he graduated from high school. He never missed one single day of school." Whatever the topic, young Hill's precocious seriousness of manner, of attention to current business, surfaced in Luffman's account. Here the subject is Hill's application to his studies: "As far as I know, he never failed to turn in a homework assignment on time. . . . This kid, from the time he was in grade school, it was work, work, work. He had his eyes on success. He was going to succeed in whatever he decided to go after. . . . He was extremely straitlaced." Later, the topic turned to churchgoing, since the Luffmans and the Hills attended the same Methodist church: "I don't know that he ever missed a Sunday school class. I did."

All this repeated stress on seriousness, combined with the honors society membership and the routine use of a middle initial in one's daily mode of address, might suggest a sense of the subject as stiff-necked and self-important before his time, the teenager as a pompous know-it-all. But nothing, apparently, could be further from the truth. Jack E. got along well with all comers, was a favorite of both students and teachers. His participation in sports didn't hurt—he was no star athlete, basketball was his only sport, but he started for two years as a forward. He was student body president in large part, according to Luffman's report, because "he knew all the high school cliques and groups and could talk easily with everybody, from the country club kids to the jocks and blue-collar types. He was probably one of the most universally liked people in the high school at that time."[3]

Fayetteville and Germany

It's not a part of the high school record, but Hill's youthful interest in military life resurfaced in college, when he enrolled in the University of Arkansas's

ROTC program, which gained him upon graduation a commission as a second lieutenant in the US Army and a two-year tour with the Eighth Infantry Division in Germany. Years later, after he found his most enduring professional home as a pioneering documentary filmmaker in his home state, Hill very often focused his work on military topics, completing a series of films on Arkansas's role in the Civil War (*War Comes to Arkansas*, *War in the Delta*, *War in the South*, and *War on the Frontier*), as well as a second group centered on the Second World War's impact in Arkansas (*Wings of Honor*, focused on the Walnut Ridge Army Flying School's training school for bomber and fighter plane pilots in Lawrence County; *Arsenal for Democracy*, chronicling the vital contributions to the war effort made by workers at Jacksonville's Arkansas Ordnance Plant; and *Faces like Ours*, exploring the experiences of both prisoners and local residents in and around the Arkansas prison camps for German and Italian POWs).

When he visited Cold War Berlin as a serviceman in 1963, Hill's reactions to its infamous wall were those of the committed neighborhood Union soldier grown older. "Nowhere can one find a better comparison of Democracy versus Communism," he wrote to the home folks, "than in Berlin. . . . The Communists have even constructed cardboard screens on the Eastern side," he continued, "so that people separated by the Wall can't even see each other. . . . One thing is certain: the Wall was not built because of any great rush of people who wanted to get in!!!"[4]

Such letters home, in their length, the scope of their distribution, and the topics addressed, convey a clear sense of large-scale plans in service to a maturing sense of important mission. At least seven installments, called "newsletters" by their author, were copied and mailed to "approximately 40" recipients between January 31, 1963, and August 20, 1964, five days before "my active tour of duty will be completed."[5] Not many twenty-four-year-olds have the confidence, or the chutzpah, to address so large a mailing list. These missives, all typewritten and single-spaced, are of considerable length—the first two are the shortest at three pages; the sixth is twice as long. They contain occasional reports of the details of soldierly life—a winter field exercise is "so cold that the water in my canteen froze"; he's "fortunate enough to be able to attend a religious retreat" in Berchtesgaden. In addition to these military and spiritual exercises, he manages to tour "the air-raid shelters and fortified bunkers used by Hitler and his personal staff."[6] He's very pleased when a water safety class he arranges for his company gains recognition in print: "We were rather flattered when articles appeared in the Division newspaper and a story was aired on the American Forces Radio Network."[7]

These incidental reports, however, are far outweighed by the same letters' detailed accounts of travels in Germany, Austria, Switzerland, and Luxembourg (the third letter mentions the purchase of a 1952 Taunus for $195 to facilitate these journeys). Later letters provide accounts of longer trips—a fifteen-day tour of Scandinavia and, above all, an eleven-day trip behind the Iron Curtain in the spring of 1964. Hill's sixth newsletter, dated May 28, 1964, is the longest of the set, mostly because of its inclusion of a two-day excerpt ("the portion from Moscow") from a forty-nine-page diary he kept on the journey. Again, as in his reports from Berlin, the visiting American serviceman sees much to confirm his Cold War perspectives. He's much impressed by the Bolshoi Theatre ("the finest concert hall I've ever been in"), and the performance of *Swan Lake* ("the first ballet I've ever seen") inspires warm thoughts: "It's really a thrilling experience hearing such great music in such an excellent setting. The thought strikes me that despite our many differences, we and the Russian audience are united through our enjoyment of *Swan Lake*."[8]

Ideological differences muted by great art resurface with a vengeance the next morning, when a visit to Moscow School Number 147 leaves the American schoolteacher's son "almost frightened" by "the way the communists use the school system as a tool to capture the minds of children." His mother is a school principal in the US and might be able to help, Hill tells an English-speaking teacher who asks about the possibility of arranging pen-pal exchanges with American students. But as the visit ends, he leaves feeling "sorry for the children we've just seen, because they are being used by the communists and don't even know it."[9]

The downhill ride continues at Lenin's tomb. "The mausoleum looks like a blockhouse and is not at all attractive," Hill notes. "In America we build beautiful white monuments to honor our national heroes. The dull red marble of the mausoleum is in sharp contrast to anything in Washington." Hill's diary preserves the moment as a climax of the trip, the scene that provides him with its summary image: "As we enter, I decide this structure is really symbolic of those things for which communism stands. It's rather spooky and cold and damp inside."[10]

This note is even more emphatic in an earlier missive's account of listening to Radio Moscow's English-language broadcasts for "entertainment" during the long night-shift hours of Operation Winter Track, the Eighth Division's 1964 winter training exercise. Surprised at the absence of "screaming attacks against the United States," Lieutenant Hill nevertheless recognizes the "subtle propaganda approach" for the ploy it is. "You see," he lectures his readers, "we maintain the peace in Europe by being ready for war, and that's why we have Operation Winter Tracks, and this is the price that we as Americans must pay if we are to stop the spread of communism."[11] Five months later, in the last of his newsletters from Europe, the same note is reiterated in Hill's account of a June trip to Ettelbruck, Luxembourg, for that town's annual General Patton Remembrance Day memorials, where his expression of thanks for generous hospitality elicited an emphatic response: "You deserve it," the young GI was told. "If it were not for America in 1917 and 1944, there would be no Luxembourg today." He was "touched" by this comment, Hill tells his readers, "because so often we are criticized today by our allies as we try to provide leadership for the Free World in the Cold War. It was so refreshing to listen to people who have not forgotten the sacrifices America has made in the past."[12]

If Hill's reports on his trips are important for their glimpses of the young soldier's political mindset, several shorter excursions inside Germany were motivated by deeply personal ties. The third newsletter, from August 19, 1963, reports two trips to Remagen, where the capture of the Ludendorff railroad bridge in March of 1945 by American First Army troops, his father, Radus Hill, among them, allowed the Allies to establish a bridgehead across the Rhine. "Whenever he reminisces about his war experiences, Remagen is usually mentioned," Hill writes. "So these were rather sentimental trips for me, knowing I was walking in the very places where my father had been under vastly different circumstances in 1945."[13]

Just under a year later, in July of 1964, "the most meaningful trip this summer in Germany" put him in his father's footsteps again. These steps had if anything been more dangerous when Dad was doing the walking than Remagen had been, because this time his son was visiting the infamous Hürtgen Forest battlefields, where Allied troops suffered more than thirty thousand casualties in a three-month offensive against outnumbered but deeply entrenched German forces. "My Dad had mailed a strip map," he writes, "and I retraced his footsteps through little towns like Lammersdorf, Simmerath, and Kesternich." A student of military history, Hill knew he walked on bloody ground: "I also explored the area around the village of Hürtgen where elements of the 8th Division took a terrible pounding. . . . On a warm sunny afternoon, it's hard to realize the horror that this entire area held for thousands of soldiers, both German and American, almost 20 years ago."[14]

Nineteen sixty-four was a year of almost constant travel. Less than a month before the trip to Russia, in February, he'd taken advantage of a four-day leave to fly to London, where he spent most of his time attending musicals (*The Sound of Music* on the first night, *How to Succeed in Business Without Really Trying* on the second, and "another production with music by Richard Rodgers, *No Strings*," on his final night). He filled the daytime hours too, managing to visit London Bridge, the Tower of London (which "really isn't a tower at all, but a large fortress"), Westminster Abbey, and "the blaze of neon signs that light Piccadilly Circus each night."[15] Later, that summer, after the trip to Russia, he joined a German tour group for a two-week trip to Scandinavia. Reporting on this journey in his final newsletter, he speaks mostly of the various capitals, calling Copenhagen "the biggest and gayest of the Scandinavian capitals," noting that "Stockholm's beauty" is so jealously guarded that a "municipal 'Beauty Council'" must "pass on the esthetic qualities of proposed buildings," and praising Oslo as "a bright, outdoorsy city" where he was most taken by the "museum containing three original Viking vessels."[16]

Even this Herculean schedule was swamped by the trips Hill undertook upon his release from active duty in August. The final newsletter, after reporting that "I've been saving for these travels ever since I've been in the Army," lays out his plans in detail: "First, I'll go to Spain and Portugal for about three weeks. Then I'll fly down to Greece and Turkey for 10 days, stopping in Vienna on my way back. Next, I plan to tour Italy and then visit Brussels, Amsterdam, and Paris." Admitting that this ambitious grand tour will "cost hundreds of dollars," he insists it is nevertheless "an opportunity I can't afford to miss."[17]

This last point may indicate something other than a now-or-never sense of urgency with regard to taking in the grand-tour spots of Europe. If Hill's travels in Germany served to connect him more deeply to his family roots by taking him backward in time, the series of international trips he undertook before and after his discharge seem designed at least in part to support developing hopes for his occupational future. These ambitions are made explicit in the paragraph immediately following the itinerary for postdemobilization travel. He'll fly back to the US around the first of November (on Uncle Sam's dime for the final transatlantic leg, he adds): "Then I'll return to school for graduate work in journalism. I hope to enter the University of Missouri and after this, I still plan to try to get a job somewhere as a radio-television newsman."[18]

A more emphatic expression of the connection between Hill's marathon travel schedule and his professional aspirations comes from a retrospective description from 1968, in a series of letters he wrote in search of a job as "a general assignment reporter for television." Describing his army years, he stresses the tie: "While overseas I used every opportunity to travel through Europe with the idea of strengthening my background for a career as a broadcast journalist." He goes on to provide details: "When I returned to the States . . . in October of 1964, I had visited almost every European country, including Russia and several of her satellites."[19]

Such plans would have come as no surprise to teachers at Rogers High School—remember the shot of the junior broadcaster at the KAMO microphone —but a closer look at the two-year arc of his military career in Germany reveals a dawning sense of specific vocation not obvious before. He'd majored in speech, after all, not journalism, as an undergraduate at the University of Arkansas, and no record survives of the high school student council member and student body president aspiring to student government positions in college. Nothing in Hill's college (or high school) record reveals any connection with school newspaper or yearbook staffs. He did join a fraternity, but a survey of 1959–62 *Razorback* yearbooks reveals a much lower profile than their high school predecessors did. For his first three years, there are only the thumbnail-size individual and fraternity photos, with captions listing his dorm residence and hometown.

The 1962 edition for his senior year features updated photos in the same two slots, but the caption line is much enlarged: "JACK EDWARD HILL," it reads, all in caps, followed by "Speech; ΣAE, Chaplain; Razorback Hall, Treasurer; Wesley Foundation; Scabbard and Blade, Vice-President; Press Club; Rogers."[20] Scabbard and Blade was and is a collegiate military honor society, and the Wesley Foundation is the campus ministry of the United Methodist Church, but Hill, though he's already an avid reader of military history and will be a devout, tithing Methodist the rest of his days, will end up as neither a clergyman nor a career military officer. No longer active as a student organization, the Press Club was established on campus in 1924 as an all-male social and public service club for journalism majors. Members helped organize a matching high school press association the following year. In 1946, the club opened its doors to women (who had established their own Pi Kappa honorary society in 1917) and disbanded soon after a student chapter of Sigma Delta Chi, a society of professional journalists, was organized in 1963. Hill's "Press Club" listing, for all its brevity, is the only hint of his future in his undergraduate career.

All this changes in Germany. When he first arrives in the winter of 1962, Hill is stationed in Baumholder, in southwestern Germany (then West Germany), as platoon leader in a mechanized rifle company, charged with a wide variety of duties. It's exciting work—he rides in helicopters and spends weeks in the field on winter training exercises—but it doesn't last long. In April 1963, he's transferred to nearby Bad Kreuznach, to a desk job providing "personnel and administrative support to the 8th Division Headquarters."[21]

He doesn't initially like it. Despite the obvious promotion—as "executive officer of the 8th Admin Company, I even have a jeep and driver at my disposal"—he misses the excitement of leading his platoon in demanding field operations and worries about the future: "I hope my new job will be as worth-while."[22] Before long, however, these worries are put to rest. The November newsletter reports that only a month after moving from Baumholder he was transferred to the division information office as troop information officer, where he's now "in charge of the 8th Infantry's radio and television efforts." No more frozen canteens or nights shivering in unheated armored personnel vehicles! (This same newsletter makes clear that this second move was actively engineered by Hill himself: "I occasionally walked next door to the Division Headquarters and dropped a few hints that if they ever needed me in the information office, I was certainly available.")[23]

The newsletters from this point on are filled with happy reports of journalistic successes. Of his radio work on the *Stage-8, Germany* show in 1963, Hill tells the home folks that "it surely has been wonderful to get back in broadcasting—if only for a few minutes each week."[24] Then, at the very end of the year, just prior to being transferred back to Baumholder, he works for nearly two months on "a documentary radio program on the history of the 8th Division." Submitted to the "key station of the American Forces Network Europe in Frankfurt," it "aired in its entirety

In his father's footsteps, Germany, 1962–64. *Photograph courtesy of Anne Hill.*

on January 4 [1964]."[25] Later the same year he reports as "the big event of the summer" a thirty-minute television documentary on tank gunnery broadcast over the armed forces television station: "The film and my narration was combined with an introduction to a tank crew who explained their jobs and told what it was like to be part of the four-man team in an M-60 tank." The tone of these reports is downright ebullient: "Of course this is the type work I enjoy most, and we've been very pleased with the comments on our presentation."[26] Nearly four years

later, back in the States and now armed with a year-
old master's degree from the University of Missouri's
School of Journalism, he's still sufficiently proud of
his armed services work to not only list it on letters
applying for jobs as a "general assignment reporter
for television" but also offer it as a sample of his talents: "I also have available the audio tapes of the documentaries I produced while in Germany."[27]

Missouri

Hill's two-year stint at the University of Missouri
was sharply focused on his professional goals. He
was awarded a William Gregory Fellowship for his
first year, 1965–66, a very generous award that would
have covered most of his costs. Hill concentrated his
course work in radio and television news, worked as
a reporter/anchor for university station KOMU-TV
and as a reporter for radio station KFRU in Columbia,
and by the time he graduated in January 1967, had
been initiated into Alpha Epsilon Rho, the national
broadcasting honorary society. His thesis was an
impressive, even groundbreaking achievement—a
171-page study of network television coverage of the
war in Vietnam, often referred to as the nation's first
televised conflict.

Hill was superbly qualified for the task. He
wrote as a graduate student in journalism, but his
own recent experience as a military information officer was fresh in his mind. As a soldier he'd worked
as a journalist, producing radio and television stories for armed services stations in Europe, and now,
returned to civilian life, he was analyzing the field's
latest technology as applied to the performance of
soldiers. Aware of the journalist's First Amendment

responsibility to provide the nation's citizenry with accurate and balanced reports from the front, he also knew firsthand the armed services' need to be sure demands for access made by news teams did not interfere with military operations. It was a situation rooted in mutual need complicated almost beyond calculation by conflicting priorities and internal rivalries in both camps. Just as the broadcast networks (and print outlets) competed among themselves for headline-grabbing stories, so the various service branches and their constituent units sought positive stories focused on their contributions to the war effort.

Hill, given his background, was perfectly placed to both understand the basic challenges of the situation and appreciate the nuances of the built-in tensions. He understood something of the geopolitical big picture—he had been to Moscow and Berlin— and as a former platoon leader who had supervised men through a bitter winter's field exercises, he also knew the ground-level world of the soldiers.

In Missouri, then, as he undertook the thesis that would be the longest piece of writing of his life, he had a greatly enlarged experience of the world under his belt. But at bottom, as his work would demonstrate, he remained the diligent, perfect-attendance student who never failed to turn in his homework on time. His seriousness of purpose is everywhere apparent. He's as convinced here as he was convinced as a platoon leader in Germany and a visitor to a Russian school of the importance of his work, its tiny but significant role, its larger geopolitical consequences. His study's first sentence identifies the then-ongoing Vietnamese conflict as "the overriding fact in the national life of the

United States," and he goes on, under an underlined "Importance of the study" heading, to note that with seventy million television sets bringing the Vietnam conflict into American homes, network news shows had "become the single most important element in the formation of public opinion." "It is no secret," he concludes, "that Peking's and Hanoi's hopes for victory in Vietnam are keyed to winning this battle of public opinion."[28] In lines like these, it's easy to see the always-earnest Hill anticipating the CV he plans as an appendix to his initial postgraduate job applications. The soldier who saw the expensive travels in Europe following his discharge as can't-afford-to-miss opportunities for professional development is here putting finishing touches on his training. Not only has he seen the world on both sides of the most geopolitically explosive axis of the day, but he's currently bringing himself up to speed on the profession's latest technologies.

The thesis itself presents a thorough, mostly descriptive account of the day-to-day work of gathering news from the Vietnam theater of operations and transporting it halfway around the world for editing and processing quickly enough for timely network broadcasts. Hill saves his study's most analytic questions for his final chapter, "Final Summary and Conclusions." Here he notes as an "overriding criticism" the charge that network coverage "has tended to place the drama of the battlefield above the cultural, political, and social implications of the war."[29] It came as no surprise to network executives that battlefield footage drew larger audiences than congressional hearings. "If it bleeds, it leads" had been a print-news staple forever. And Hill is simply reporting a basic fact of the business when he notes almost in passing that "the fireworks at CBS over live coverage of the hearings pointed out once again the commercial-entertainment side is in control of network TV and, therefore, has the last word."[30] In fact, the very issues Hill confronts in abstract terms in his master's thesis—the push and pull between newspapers and broadcast news operations as commercial ventures and the fourth-estate social responsibilities of journalists—would in the not-so-distant future be encountered as central concerns in the day-to-day performance of his job.

They are not central to his investigations, and there was no way he could have known their significance at the time, but passages in Hill's thesis where senior correspondents worry out loud about the new reporters who came in with the television crews now seem spectacularly dated. They seemed to the veterans a motley crew, strikingly young, oddly unprofessional, disturbingly undeferential. "New York has, on occasion, sent misfits," complained one, "people whose jobs were in jeopardy at home." They were, he concluded, "an odd assortment of many nationalities —adventurers from all over the world."[31]

No doubt they were all these things, but with the advantage of a half century's retrospect, it's clear just this cohort ended up producing that bizarre conflict's most vivid accounts. The most obvious instance in the world of print would be Michael Herr's *Dispatches*, not published until 1977 but by 1998 already enshrined as the closing section in the canonical gold-standard Library of America two-volume *Reporting Vietnam* set. Other enduring accounts were produced by photographers Larry Burrows, Dickey Chapelle, Catherine Leroy, and Tim Page; by cartoonists Tony Auth, Herbert "Herblock"

Block, and a still-feisty Bill Mauldin; and by Armed Forces Network DJ Adrian Cronauer, the real-life model for Robin Williams's breakout role in *Good Morning, Vietnam*. But the perfect emblems for the dark, hallucinatory aura of the whole misguided nightmare would have to be photojournalists Sean Flynn and Dana Stone, who in an Asian reprise of the previous year's blockbuster *Easy Rider* rode off on motorcycles in search of a story about American operations along the Cambodian border in 1970 and were never heard from again.

Jack Hill was far from this scruffy and dangerous world, a very buttoned-up graduate student earnestly researching a thesis, but even his sober enterprise is occasionally pulled into the era's disorienting orbit. Addressing the relationship between the press corps and military information officers, he sugarcoats his presentation with a generally upbeat lead: "The TV veterans have unanimous praise for the cooperation available at every level," but it's not long before he's reporting that "the daily briefings in Saigon have become better known . . . as the 'five o'clock follies.'" Reporters just back from field expeditions, he concludes, often found "that they knew more than the information officer."[32]

Overall, the thesis is a thoroughly impressive piece of work on a subject lacking a guiding body of prior scholarship, and Hill's University of Missouri mentors no doubt felt amply justified in their choice for the Gregory Fellowship. He would never attempt another project of such length and scope. Twenty years later, however, bruised by hard experience but still wholly unbowed, he would return to the general topic of journalism's responsibilities and the obstacles to their effective accomplishment. In a forty-page essay titled "Unequal Justice Under the Law: And the Arkansas Media's Role in It," not quite one-fourth the length of his thesis and a good deal darker in tone, written in what the author clearly regards as the rubble of defeat, he would restate his view of journalism's basic task. For all its greater brevity, the essay would be less coherent than the neophyte's thesis. It would overstate its case, and the note of personal grievance would undermine its authority. It would never be published, and even if it had been, it would have come across as a valedictory screed, a good-bye and good riddance to a statewide journalistic culture too venal to deserve loyalty. The author was down and out but as it happened just getting started in the two-decade career in documentary film that would bring his most lasting renown.[33]

Denver, Jackson, Dallas

A series of short-term jobs served as Hill's introduction to full-time professional work. The first of these was with station KLZ in Denver, Colorado. Hired as a radio deskman, he was soon dissatisfied with the lack of opportunities for on-air experience. What had worked in the army, when he "walked next door" and managed to arrange his own transfer from administrative to information services duties, worked less well in Denver. In less than a year, he was sending out letters in search of better opportunities, casting his net widely. Most of his time at KLZ had "been spent writing material for others," he wrote to a news director in Tampa, Florida. "Even though KLZ has a tremendous reputation for news, its high rating isn't helping to advance my own career in broadcasting." Stations in Miami, Montgomery,

Nashville, Oklahoma City, Shreveport, and Tulsa, among others, received similar queries, the written equivalent of cold calls in that he was typically not responding to a specific job listing. "And so I write this letter," he tells the man in Tampa, "not knowing if you have any openings on your news staff, but hoping that a person with my background is the type of journalist you are seeking."[34]

Some of these letters paid off, with editors requesting the work samples he offered from his time at KLZ, as well as earlier efforts from his time in the army. Responding to one of these requests from the news director at station WSFA-TV in Montgomery, Alabama, Hill is more forthcoming than he was in his initial pitch letters. He's been fired from KLZ, he reports, and then goes on to detail his sense of what led to his dismissal: "The unemotional way in which I carried out my responsibilities" was mistaken for "a lack of aggressiveness." The passage concludes with Hill's admitting he's given "my side of the story" and explicitly mentioning the possibility that the folks considering him in Montgomery might wish to contact his boss at KLZ "to get his side."[35] This letter is on its face an extraordinary piece of unsparing self-analysis from a job applicant of twenty-seven dealing head on with what may have been his first experience of defeat. Hill, after all, had basked in what seems in retrospect an unbroken string of triumphs, winning everything from high school elective offices and athletic championships to military promotions and graduate school fellowships. But then, in his initial foray into the real-world workforce in his chosen occupation, the golden boy finds himself summarily fired after barely a year at his entry-level job.

Persistence and what Hill may have understood

as forthrightness eventually paid off. Good fortune held—less than a month after the confessional letter to Alabama, the fledgling journalist run out of Denver was hired at WLBT-WJDX, the NBC affiliate in Jackson, Mississippi. A letter dated April 19, 1968, written from Denver, thanks news director Dave Mieher for hosting his two-day visit and for "hiring me as an addition to the news staff." The letter closes on a note of high optimism: "I think you are providing me with the very opportunity I need for future success in radio-TV news."[36]

Such future triumphs, when they came, arrived on several fronts at almost the same time. On February 10, 1971, just short of the three-year anniversary of Hill's hopeful thank-you message, Mieher received another letter. WLBT, he was told, had been "chosen as one of the National Finalists for the 1970 Station Award presented by The National Academy of Television Arts and Sciences" for its hour-long documentary program *Homes like These*, narrated and produced by Hill.[37] As a finalist for this award, popularly known as an Emmy, Hill and his Jackson employers were in good company—the ten finalists included shows produced in much larger markets (Boston, Philadelphia, Chicago, Houston, Phoenix, and Los Angeles, among others). Mieher was invited to attend or have a representative at the academy's national convention in March, where the winner would hoist the statuette and all finalists would receive plaques.

This nomination and the film that garnered it were impressive accomplishments. The Jackson *Clarion-Ledger* and the Lamar Insurance Company's in-house publication carried laudatory accounts (Lamar owned WLBT, the final three letters standing for Lamar Broadcast Television), and Hill got yet another local-boy-makes-good story in the *Rogers Daily News*. For the Jackson station, the nomination arrived as validation, proof that a local news team could produce work that stood up to comparison with the big hitters on the coasts. For Hill it was personal—it meant that, given the opportunity, he could script and front long-form programs that came across as both informative and engaging, good news work and good television. *Homes like These* was a major undertaking, more than a year in the making and shot in thirteen locations ranging from Gulfport on the southern coast to Tupelo in the north. It was controversial too—low-income housing was a hot-button issue then as now, complicated by class and racial tensions. Hill got angry letters.

Meanwhile, just as these stories and his regular appearances on local newscasts were putting Hill in Jackson's public eye, his private life was taking a marked turn for the better. Sometime in April of 1971, according to her recollection, he met his future wife, Anne Powers, through the good offices of a local church singles group. "I chased him unmercifully," she recalled, adding that she originally got his name wrong. "I didn't watch WLBT, but my mother did. I asked her if she knew a reporter on WLBT named Jack Hillhouse. She laughed and corrected me." The merciless pursuit opened decorously enough: "I remember inviting him over to my house for dinner for our first 'date,' so to speak. It was his birthday, which was on May 18."[38] A meeting in church, followed by a first date where you meet the folks, sample the home cooking, even as the plaudits for your first award-nominated film roll in—Hill must have experienced all this as a reassuring return to the most-likely-to-succeed fast lane after the rocky beginning in Denver.

By the beginning of 1973, roughly eighteen months after their initial meeting, the new couple was engaged. They would marry in August, with the groom's father serving as best man and high school pal Mack Luffman joining *Homes like These* cameraman Carroll Fulgham as groomsmen. The former classmate found much to recognize in the more grown-up version of his old friend: "We tried getting him to laugh at his wedding. The grooms-men did all the typical things. In Jackson we found a bookstore that sold pornographic magazines, and we stuffed them in his suitcase. Never even got a grin. He was just as straitlaced as they come."[39] This stiff-necked, formal posture to the world was also noted at the office. Fulgham, who worked well with Hill and respected his abilities, recalled him as so "super pro-fessional" in his demeanor that colleagues teased him with unusual relish when he once got tongue tied and referred to "women's lib" as "lemons wib" over the air. "Other reporters would have just laughed it off, but Jack was really embarrassed," Fulgham said. "He was always serious about his work."[40]

For all the surface triumph of this period, how-ever, life in Jackson and at WLBT was often difficult. "Jack was ahead of his time in Jackson," noted his bride, raised from birth in the city and educated in its schools. "He was there during the times of racial tension and for many folks Jack was on the wrong side."[41] "Racial tension" drastically understates the case. How much Hill knew of this history when he accepted Dave Mieher's offer is unclear, but Jackson in general and WLBT in particular in the era leading up to his arrival is accurately described as an epicenter

Father, mother, bride, and groom, Jackson, Mississippi, 1973.
Photograph courtesy of Anne Hill.

of segregationist resistance to the civil rights movement. When NAACP Mississippi field secretary
Medgar Evers was assassinated in 1963, gunned
down in his Jackson driveway by white supremacist
Klansman Byron De La Beckwith, the local newspaper's headline called Beckwith a Californian despite
the fact that he'd lived in Mississippi since he was six.

WLBT, during the same period, served as the
central broadcast outlet for segregationist voices.
The infamous White Citizens' Council operated a
bookstore in the lobby of the station's office building

(station manager Fred Beard was a member), and national NBC news feeds featuring civil rights stories were routinely scrubbed from local broadcasts—a "Sorry, Cable Trouble" placard appeared when substitute programming could not be found quickly enough. A particularly egregious instance occurred in 1955, when NBC's *Brown v. Board of Education* stories featuring Thurgood Marshall were cut from WLBT coverage. African American viewers complained that the only way a black man could get on television in Jackson was to get arrested, and it was noted that a local weatherman's pronunciation of "Negro," the then-current "polite" racial term of reference, often edged toward openly derisive N-word enunciation. In 1962, the station aired editorials opposing the admission of James Meredith to the University of Mississippi, and on June 20, 1969, just over a year into Hill's tenure, WLBT became one of only two stations ever to have its license revoked for racial bias violations under the FCC's "fairness doctrine." WLBT existed in an administrative limbo until 1978, when it was licensed to new ownership headed by Clarksdale civil rights activist Aaron Henry.[42]

That tensions were present in the day-to-day operations of WLBT during Hill's time there is evident from his surviving papers. One issue had to do with royalties paid by other stations for footage shot by locals. Cameraman Fulgham recalled that these were treated at the beginning as private transactions between outside users and the staffers. He remembered being approached by BBC reporters to arrange use of "extra footage" of "some civil rights meeting" at the state capitol, where coverage of the legislature was Hill's primary assignment. At some point, however, Mieher ordered such revenues shared among the whole news staff. "That wasn't really fair," Fulgham concluded, adding that Mieher generally "took a hard look at the world."[43]

Another issue had to do with station rules regarding editorializing by reporters and anchors. This one involved Hill directly, and he was quick to make his voice heard. On April 14, 1969, almost exactly a year after his arrival, he addressed a memorandum to station manager Bob McRaney Jr. arguing for a distinction between a voice speaking for the station itself and "commentary" clearly identified with a single reporter offered to contextualize unfolding stories. A sample of what he intended survives as a script for a boycott story from Canton. Hill's "commentary" runs to more than three sentences, and its openly hortatory tone highlights the reporter's determination to play a positive role. Opening with a rhetorical question—"Does a general economic boycott . . . serve the best interest of *all* the people?"—Hill promptly provides a negative answer. It's obvious that no boycott serves the interests of targeted merchants, but Hill argues that the "need for watch-dog committees, along with threats and intimidations to maintain the boycott," cause it also to fail the interests of the protesting community. Boycotts also fail to "improve race relations," according to Hill, because "for while a boycott may cause some physical barriers to fall, . . . in the long run it tends to harden the barriers within the minds of men." The "responsible answer," the reporter concludes, falls back on the familiar need for "communication between the races"—that is, talk, presumably while continuing to spend money with the merchants responsible for the "physical barriers."[44]

This little "commentary" comes across today as a spineless sermonette, craven in its accommodation of segregationist custom, powerful now only for what it suggests of the entrenched powers arrayed against the boycotters. But even so timid a recognition as this of the protesters' perspective was at that time and in that place an act of some courage. Hill had been to Berlin and Moscow, he'd led Cold War troops in winter field exercises, but he's on tiptoe in Mississippi, wearing kid gloves, walking scared.

Even as the *Homes like These* award nomination was celebrated in press releases and news stories, then, there were signs of discontent in the newsroom. It was clearly a time of transition. The old days of the station as an unapologetic mouthpiece for the White Citizens' Council had ended. Fred Beard and the announcer with pronunciation issues (his name was Bob Neblett) were gone, and the station was hiring African American staff members. Corrice Collins, who in the late 1960s became WLBT's first minority anchor, was already there when Hill arrived. Hill became, by Fulgham's report, "kind of his teacher" to Collins, and Anne Hill remembers her husband encouraging Collins to pursue graduate studies in journalism at his own alma mater.[45]

Another groundbreaking African American hire was Randall Pinkston, who was hired in 1971 and later established a celebrated career at CBS.

All these modestly progressive moves were at the time controversial within the station's management. Even the Emmy-nominated documentary was accomplished in the teeth of in-house resistance. Mieher was "not a fan at first," according to Fulgham's report. A good bit of *Homes like These* was shot as "extra footage" on other assignments—several shacks seen in the final cut were shot "almost within sight" of the capitol and WLBT offices.

Then, on January 29, 1971, less than two weeks before the arrival of Mieher's congratulatory letter from the National Academy, Fulgham, the cameraman on the acclaimed film, was fired, and divisions in the newsroom staff were pushed into the open. A two-page, single-spaced memorandum dated one week later and addressed to "Management" cites Fulgham's dismissal as an appropriate occasion for general discussion of "serious morale problems throughout the station." At the center of these, the memorandum suggests, is a "double-standard" in treatment of staff members from "two camps—the old guys, the ones who were here prior to 1968—and the new guys, the ones who came during and after that year." The "old guys" are described as better treated, with lighter work assignments and more relaxed supervision: "Management will tolerate things from the old guys that are not tolerated from the rest of us. A serious failure by an old guy can go largely unnoticed. But a less serious shortcoming by a new guy can be dealt with harshly." One sentence may single out news director Mieher as a slacker: "We are not yet to the point where we can afford the luxury of even a news director who is told he is to do little but supervise."[46]

Hill, who surely participated in writing the memorandum since he still had a copy in his papers forty years later, devoted himself with considerable energy to public service broadcasting in Jackson. His reaction to virulent racism and rear-guard segregationist resistance to integration brought a new note of protest to his work. *Homes like These* drew hostile audience reactions for a reason—several

Natchez viewers found offensive the juxtaposition of local slums to the lavishly restored antebellum plantation homes that were the city's pride. Back in Jackson in the spring of 1971, Hill organized and served as moderator for a panel discussion specifically addressed to the desegregation of local schools. Titled "Desegregation: Students Tell It like It Is," the program featured comments from ten students, evenly divided by race, from Jackson's five high schools. "We got into their feelings about the educational environment, problems of discipline, how they felt about news coverage of desegregation, and what they'd learned," Hill told a reporter from the *Jackson Daily News*. The hour-long discussion was filmed and broadcast over WLBT on June 1.[47]

By the end of 1971, Hill's frustration with WLBT policies and internal rivalries in the newsroom had reached a breaking point. He wanted out. Anne Hill remembers a general desire for a bigger market and a specific application for a position about as far from Jackson as he could go without a passport: "He flew out to Seattle for an interview but he didn't get the job. Then WFAA came along. . . . I think Jack moved to Dallas in early 1972. . . . We were engaged in January of 1973 and had a big church wedding on August 4, 1973."[48]

The booming Texas metropolis certainly filled the bill as a larger market than Jackson, but it wasn't the capital, so covering the state legislature as his primary day-to-day responsibility, as he'd done in Mississippi, was no longer possible. WFAA ran a large news operation, widely admired for cutting-edge use of new technologies, and Hill worked a wide range of stories. One of the biggest brought him back to Arkansas to report on the challenging efforts to recover the bodies of eleven passengers and crew from the crash of Texas International Airlines Flight 655 on a mountain near Mena in September 1973. A draft of Hill's report from the Mena airport survives in his papers, as do scripts from an in-depth five-part series on fiscal, environmental, and social costs of traffic congestion in Dallas. There is also a three-ring binder filled with newspaper clippings focused on the Texas races in the general election of 1972. The piece from Mena is written not as a hard news story—the plane had flown far off course and crashed in remote terrain, with the wreckage undiscovered for three days—but as a somber account, elegiac in tone, of difficult and dangerous work done in the aftermath of tragedy. Bodies were recovered by military helicopters working from makeshift landing zones on steep mountainsides.[49]

The traffic congestion series was very different; filled with data and buttressed by statements from various experts, it addressed the issue from many angles, moving adroitly within broadcast journalism's tight time constraints between statistical generalities and down-on-the-ground anecdotes showing their effects on local citizens. One especially effective segment focused on difficulties faced in a freeway-centered urban street system by poor and elderly people without automobiles or unable to drive them.[50] In Dallas as in Jackson, Hill's work showed a steadily increasing concern with the treatment of society's most vulnerable people.

Anne didn't move to Dallas until the fall of 1973, after their August marriage. They moved into an apartment in the Oak Lawn area of North Dallas, launching their life together with little sense of the challenges ahead. These arrived promptly and from several points. Anne was still writing wedding gift thank-you cards when Jack, just returned from the plane-crash trip to Mena, came home to report that newly hired news director Marty Haag had called him aside as he was leaving to tell him he was being fired. Hill wasn't alone—Haag had been hired to revamp WFAA's news operation, then running third in the fight for viewers among Dallas stations, and he was overseeing a wholesale restructuring of the news staff. It brought no consolation to Hill, fired for the second time, in his third job, but Haag's efforts proved spectacularly successful at WFAA—he hired a hotshot trio away from KWTV in Oklahoma City and soon had WFAA's news programming dominating local ratings.[51]

On the surface this sounds like a repeat of the Denver experience—an aggressive news director assessing Hill's reserved demeanor as a lack of energy and drive. But this time the results were close to catastrophic. The blows kept coming too, a second right on the heels of the first. "I went out looking for a job the very next day," Anne recalls, adding that the president of Jackson's Deposit Guaranty National Bank was helpful in recommending her. "But then, on my first day on that job, Jack telephoned to say we'd gotten a call from Jackson. My mother was in the hospital, diagnosed with terminal lung cancer." Bride and groom, just-hired bank employee and just-fired television journalist, drove immediately to Jackson, but when they met with doctors there, the news only got worse. "They said she had maybe six months to live, and they weren't far off. Then, as a kind of last straw, when we walked out of the hospital, we saw that somebody had smashed into our car in the parking lot. A hit-and-run. What else could go wrong? We did get to spend Christmas with my mother that year— she took the bus to Dallas because she was afraid to fly. But then she went downhill very fast in the spring of 1974. She died in May. Those were tough times."[52]

The ignominious end to his employment at WFAA, coupled with the earlier setback in Denver and the unsettled situation in the newsroom at WLBT, apparently rattled Hill's confidence in his career choice. He helped make ends meet in Dallas by driving a cab—he didn't know the street grid well enough to pass the exam for a general license, so he drove routes connecting the airports (Love Field at first and then the just-opened Dallas/Fort Worth Regional Airport) to area hotels. "Jack wondered at the time if the television news business was going to work out for him," Anne said. "While he was driving the cab, he explored a position producing in-house films for Bell Helicopter, but that didn't work out either."[53]

Somehow, driving the cab, working in the bank, living in a town that was home to neither of them, and dealing with the illness and death of Anne's mother, the couple made it through the first year of their marriage. They were surviving day to day, with a sharpened sense of the world's potential for disaster and little sense of what the future might hold. They had no way of knowing, as 1974 turned to 1975, that a television station manager in the rural flatlands of Northeast Arkansas was looking hard for a news director. Jonesboro was not the bigger market Hill was looking for when he left Jackson, but news work anywhere beat driving a cab from day one, and as it turned out, the station there would offer him the best opportunities yet to make realities of his large ambitions.

CHAPTER 2

HIGH TIMES AND BIG TROUBLE

A New Start in Jonesboro

The station manager with hiring on his mind was Darrel Cunningham, himself just installed in his position. KAIT was itself a relatively new kid on the broadcast-communications block, a family operation owned by George T. Hernreich, who also owned stations in Fayetteville and his hometown of Fort Smith. "They said I would not last ninety days," a triumphant Hernreich recalled in a film clip aired in 1988 as part of the station's twenty-fifth anniversary celebrations.[1] His Jonesboro station took to the air in 1963, without a network affiliation and running on mostly used equipment. Interviewed for a 1981 newspaper feature, Cunningham recalled that the "station struggled pretty hard for a couple of years."[2] Live wrestling matches were marred by occasional glitches—an overzealous fan in the studio audience once interrupted a bout, clubbing the "heel" with a chair before being chased into the parking lot by the now genuinely enraged grappler.[3]

More successful was a country music show called *The Gene Williams Country Junction Show* ("Great big howdy to ya. Welcome to our little country show," says a tuxedo-clad Gene). Its studio audiences were better behaved, and area musicians happy to perform were in good supply. The fledgling station filled out this helter-skelter schedule with Hollywood reruns. The first day's broadcast, on July 15, set a pattern, opening with a midafternoon newscast followed by a screening of *The Indian Fighter*, a 1955 western with Kirk Douglas in the saddle.[4]

The network affiliation with ABC was signed in 1965, though fiscal irregularities—bribes or blackmail, depending on who was paying which barrister—left a cloud on the station's license for more than a decade. In 1969 Hernreich's son, Bob, economics master's degree in hand, arrived with plans for an upgrade. "I got to know Bob Hernreich about 1971," Cunningham recalled. "At the time I was assistant professor of radio-TV at Arkansas State University in Jonesboro." Persuading the young academic to forgo a campus career took some time—Cunningham was busy teaching full-time while working toward a doctorate at Ohio University, but Hernreich eventually prevailed. "I had to wait a year to complete the program and the additional required teaching at Arkansas State, and I joined the station in July 1974."[5]

Less than a year later Jack Hill came calling, in answer to a job description placed in *Broadcasting* magazine by Cunningham. That was "what you did in those days," he recalled in a 2018 interview, "if you were looking for employees in the broadcasting business." Hill's letter was impressive, and Cunningham also liked the Arkansas roots and the University of Missouri degree, so he invited Hill to Jonesboro for an interview. "My wife and I drove over and met Jack's flight," Cunningham recalled. "It's about an hour, hour and fifteen minutes, from the Memphis airport back to Jonesboro, and we've laughed since then about that time because we asked Jack a question or two and then he did a monologue the rest of the way back. But it was an interesting monologue!"[6]

It must have been. Cunningham hired Hill as anchor of a three-man team, pairing him with weatherman Terry Wood and sports reporter Dick Clay. They made an appealing on-air trio. Wood was a former disc jockey who "had no meteorological training to speak of but had a charming personality and a great on-camera way about him," according to Cunningham's recollections. Clay, on the sports desk, "was kind of in the middle," but where Hill was "Mr. Serious, Mr. All Business," Wood was affable and relaxed. "Terry would tease him and joke about him," Cunningham recalled. "They just made perfect foils. People loved them." It hadn't hurt, either, that Hill's monologue likely included references to his investigative work in Jackson and Dallas, since Cunningham had his own interest in long-form research-based stories. If as station manager he understood solid local and regional news coverage as crucial to a television station's role in its community, he also thought of investigative reporting as a basic component of good journalism. "Jack was a person who wanted to do it, had the talent to do it," Cunningham remembered. "It turned out to be a really good fit."[7]

He didn't emphasize it in conversations with his newly hired news director—"Jack didn't know a whole lot about that . . . he had plenty to do with his work"—but Cunningham had additional incentives in encouraging Hill's commitment to serious investigative pieces: "There was another motive in the back of my mind—this had to do with the station's license."

When Hill arrived in 1975, KAIT had been operating for nine years on a temporary permit while appealing its license revocation, and Cunningham was eager to build up evidence of reputable performance, especially in the news department. "Every time Jack Hill won an award, we immediately fired a letter to our Washington attorney. . . . To this day I believe that the work Jack Hill did not only brought prestige to the station but probably saved the license."[8]

A good case might be made for Cunningham's latter claim—the station's permanent license was restored in 1978—but the first one, on the matter of prestige, is beyond doubt, as Hill wasted no time seizing the opportunities Cunningham offered. Hill's smooth working relationship with news desk colleagues Clay and Wood was matched by his compatibility on field shoots with cameraman Ray Scales. Like Hill, Scales was a college-educated Arkansan with a stint in the military in his background—born in Tyronza, he had graduated from high school in nearby Marked Tree and majored in English at Arkansas Agricultural, Mechanical and Normal College (now the University of Arkansas at Pine Bluff) before being drafted into the US Army. After completing his hitch in 1971, he was hired as KAIT's first African American employee. "What Bob Hernreich told me when he hired me—he said, 'You're not a token,'" Scales remembered. "I was relentless. I wanted to work." After brief stints writing commercials and covering sports—"I didn't want to do that; I wanted to be out and about, where the action was"— Scales found his niche as a photographer.[9]

"Steve Cohen [another newly hired reporter and photographer] came in one day and said, 'Do you want to shoot?'" Scales recalled. "I said, 'I don't know how.'" They sent him anyway, one Saturday, with predictable results: "We went out, and that video was terrible. It was jerking all around!" But Scales was eager to learn and soon had his bosses on board: "Shortly thereafter, Bob Hernreich came to me, said, 'We're gonna send you to Kodak film school.'" Training behind him, Scales returned to Jonesboro as a staff photographer at KAIT. When Hill arrived in 1975, Scales was ready:

> RAY SCALES. When Jack came, what he did, he
>   perfected it. Dick Clay showed me a lot of stuff
>   too. I kind of took my time, and I would learn.
> BECKY ALLISON. So Jack took you to still another
>   level?
> SCALES. Yes, he did. . . . When Jack came, he
>   would notice little details. Do this angle here.
>   Go low here, and go high there. And then,
>   what we would do, we would edit together, and
>   he would show me stuff. So I will always give
>   him credit for that.[10]

Paired with Scales, Hill produced multiple award-winning long-form pieces right out of the gate. One of the first was a 1976 piece examining county jail conditions in KAIT's Northeast Arkansas viewing area that earned the station's first (Hill's second) Emmy nomination from the National Academy of Television Arts and Sciences. Another nomination arrived just a year later, for *Is There Any Hope for Hope Street?*, a Jonesboro-based reprise of *Homes like These* exposing woeful conditions in low-income rental homes in Jonesboro. It also won the Public Service Award for 1977 from Arkansas Women in Radio and Television, placed third in the public service reporting category of Sigma Delta Chi Society of Professional Journalists' national awards contest, and earned a Citation of Special Merit from the Robert F. Kennedy Journalism Awards competition.

By the time the Hills traveled together to Virginia in May of 1978 to pick up the latter award at the home of Ethel Kennedy, they surely sensed a turn in their fortunes. Anne had landed a good job at Jonesboro's Citizens Bank, the couple had purchased a house, and they were welcomed members of the congregation at Huntington Avenue United Methodist Church. The days of driving cabs, of editors sensing in Jack a too-wooden, insufficiently aggressive journalist, were fading memories. The man from Northwest Arkansas and the woman from Jackson, Mississippi, had found a home halfway between.

Times of Triumph

Cunningham's KAIT team, headed by Hill and Scales, followed up its early successes on the awards front with a steady string of winners in the late 1970s and early 1980s. *Crisis at the Crossings*, a 1978 exploration of the high incidence of accidents at the many Northeast Arkansas railroad crossings lacking lights or gates, picked up a citation from the Alfred I. duPont–Columbia University journalism awards and won a Broadcast Media Award from San Francisco State University. Nineteen seventy-nine saw Hill and a three-man KAIT news team earn a $2,500 runner-up prize from the Media Awards for Economic Understanding for their report on the decline of family farms, *How 'Ya Gonna Keep 'Em Down on the Farm . . . after They've Gone Broke?*

Stories centered on farming were an obvious focus in Northeast Arkansas, where agricultural

operations played a central role in the region's econ-
omy, so it comes as no surprise that KAIT produced
several additional special programs on closely
related topics. *Intensive Agriculture: The Other Side*
picked up a Champion Media Award for Economic
Understanding from Dartmouth College's Amos Tuck
School of Business Administration in 1983, while
Black Farmers in Arkansas: A Tradition Disappears,
broadcast in 1984, examined the 98 percent drop in
the number of African American farmers in the state
since 1930.

Perhaps the most successful special program
from the early work of the KAIT teams was *The
Economics of Water*, focused on the falling water
table in the delta counties of Arkansas. Aired in
November of 1981, it won the "AG Oscar" award, "one
of agricultural journalism's most coveted prizes,"
according to a congratulatory story in the *Jonesboro
Sun*. Hill is pictured next to a gushing water pipe and
quoted in the story; Ray Scales and three other staff
members who worked on the program are also cred-
ited.[11] *The Economics of Water* also won the station's
first Champion Media Award and a second duPont-
Columbia. Almost forty years after the fact, Scales
has vivid recollections of working on it. A deeply
devout man who for forty years has pastored Baptist
congregations in the area, he worried at the time
that a recent surgery would impair his camerawork:
"I prayed the whole time we were shooting that documentary," he said. "God was unveiling those shots to
me. While I was shooting, something just happened
and I was on it, you know?" One sequence in particular stood out: "We were doing this one shot, this
irrigation thing, shooting water down in the ground,
and they were harvesting soybeans. There were these

combines coming by, and the water was coming up to this combine. God did it. God focused that shot. It was a perfect shot."[12]

It would be misleading, despite the prominence of these programs, to describe KAIT's news coverage as dominated by agricultural topics. During the same late 1970s–early 1980s period, the station produced in-depth special reports on the lack of adequate medical care in the region's communities (*Is There a Doctor in the Town?* from 1982), problems associated with alcohol use (*We've Been Drinking on the Railroad* from 1984), and corruption in area law enforcement offices. The pieces on the latter topic were spectacularly successful in award competitions. *And Justice for All?*, a 1980 series exposing malfeasance in the office of Poinsett County sheriff Gerald T. Crawford, was an especially big winner, earning a National Headliner Award for outstanding public service from the Press Club of Atlantic City, New Jersey, and an investigative reporting award from Investigative Reporters and Editors (IRE), a professional journalists' association headquartered in Hill's old School of Journalism at the University of Missouri. It was also one of three finalists for a Sigma Delta Chi Society of Professional Journalists Award for distinguished service in journalism.

I Run This County, from 1985, scored a second award from IRE and was certainly the most controversial of Hill's KAIT pieces. A long time in the making, it focused on a wide range of spectacularly corrupt practices in the operations of the sheriff's office of St. Francis County. The sheriff at the center, a flamboyant figure named Coolidge Conlee, was not happy with Hill's inquiries, and he did not go down easily. Not six months after *I Run This County* aired, on June 8, 1985, Hill and his graduate student cameraman were assaulted by a deputy sheriff while pursuing additional leads on the story, and the following year Sheriff Conlee sued the journalist for $7.5 million. Anne Hill got intimidating calls at home. The voices of strangers urged her to tell her husband to back off. "We know where you live," they said.

In the teeth of this array of physical attacks, verbal harassments, and legal threats, the Hills and KAIT persevered and eventually prevailed. Conlee was turned out of office in 1986, was indicted and convicted in 1988, and drew a twenty-year sentence. Sheriff Crawford, up in Poinsett County, was less pugnacious in his opposition, though he did sue KAIT for $1.5 million in 1980, complaining the *And Justice for All* reports were "false, malicious, and fabricated."[13] Both suits were ultimately dropped. Remembering the protracted episodes forty years later, Cunningham noted with satisfaction that "none of the lawsuits resulted in judgments against Jack or the station."[14]

Not all special programs centered on such hard news investigations—*Rise Up and Live*, for example, appeared in 1979 and won a Gabriel Awards Certificate of Merit from the National Catholic Association for Broadcasters. It was described in an *Arkansas Gazette* story on KAIT's successes as

> about as "soft" as a news program can be and still rate as news. It opened with a look at two tiny "storefront" churches in Jonesboro, one of which meets in an abandoned drive-in movie theater. There was a segment on a black woman who is the pastor for four rural churches in the area, and one on the activities of Temple Israel, Jonesboro's small but active Jewish congregation. The last half of the program was an examination of

Heifer Project International, a Little Rock–based nondenominational project that supplies farm animals to families in underdeveloped countries. Hill and cameraman Ray Scales traveled along with a shipment of animals to Guatemala to record the impact the program had on its recipients.[15]

As these national-level prizes rolled in from university journalism departments and national press and broadcast associations on both coasts, Cunningham, Hill, and their newsroom colleagues found themselves invited to award banquets and other ceremonies analogous to the Hills' journey to the home of Ethel Kennedy in 1978. One of the biggest invitations came relatively early, when *Crisis at the Crossings* picked up its duPont-Columbia citation. In February 1978, Hill and Cunningham traveled to New York for ceremonies the station manager remembered vividly forty years later: "It was quite a moment. We were put up at the Waldorf Astoria. Jack is called up for his piece, and Robert MacNeil of the *MacNeil/Lehrer Report* hands out the award."[16] Hill would return to New York in 1982 and 1983, both times to collect awards for *The Economics of Water*. On the latter trip, he would make his most high-profile television appearance, as an honoree on the April 4 edition of *The Phil Donahue Show*. Arkansas audiences caught him on Fort Smith and Little Rock stations, and Hill's papers preserve a congratulatory letter from Jonesboro bank president Walter DeRoeck, who noted that his wife was furious over the failure of the *Jonesboro Sun* to carry notice of the local anchor's star turn.

Hill was on the other side of the continent in

1981, attending the national conference of Investigative Reporters and Editors in San Diego, where *And Justice for All* won its IRE Award for its "dramatic report on a rural sheriff, whose improprieties . . . led to his defeat at the polls after four terms in office."[17] He also served on a panel at this meeting, holding forth at the "Television's Startime" session, where the conference program promised "top winners in investigative reporting for television will 'show and tell' how they did it."[18] In 1986, Hill served on two more panels, the first at the IRE Conference in Portland, Oregon, where he picked up the award for *I Run This County* and spoke on "Corrupt Sheriffs" at a June 27 panel session. The same year saw him in San Antonio for an IRE regional conference, where on October 4 he was a panelist for a discussion called "Starting Small: The Low-Budget Investigation."

Small was an understatement—beginning in 1975, after Hill was hired, the station inaugurated a once-a-year news special, then doubled the number to two starting in 1979 to have one for each rating period. "The programs are produced on a shoestring," an *Arkansas Gazette* story reported in the latter year. "The news department is allowed only $1,000 for each program—and each one does double duty: it first is shown as a series, in short segments on the regular 6 p.m. and 10 p.m. newscasts, and then is edited into one 27-minute program that is shown intact, without commercial sponsorship."[19]

Cunningham's recollections fill in the picture: "Maybe it would be a five-part series, two or maybe three minutes for each part, run during the ratings week so we'd get the credit." Combined and reedited, the same material would constitute the special program: "We would preempt the six-thirty sitcom, whatever it was, and run it right after the news as a thirty-minute special at the conclusion of the week, typically on a Friday."[20]

Meanwhile, KAIT's local programming was racking up jaw-dropping numbers in viewing-share ratings. By the spring of 1981, a feature article in the Memphis *Commercial Appeal*'s Sunday television insert was describing KAIT's market share as "phenomenal": "KAIT-TV's 6 p.m. news in the November 1979 Arbitron sweep had a 58 ADI (area of dominant influence) rating . . . 'the highest figure recorded by any program . . . on any U.S. television station.'"[21] Cunningham explained:

> There are two numbers that are significant. One is rating—the percentage of the total market. The share is your percentage of the sets that are actually watching something. . . . If you lived in Imboden, Arkansas, or Pocahontas, you probably didn't get much off the air except Channel 8 in Jonesboro. Probably not Little Rock. Probably not Springfield, Missouri, or Cape Girardeau. . . .
>
> In Jonesboro, Memphis was certainly well within range, but west of Jonesboro—that's where Memphis started to fade. We had a niche in that area.[22]

During this same period, Hill and Cunningham, utilizing their ties with KATV, their sister ABC affiliate, would drive to Little Rock to do interviews for KAIT's public affairs programs. One of these trips, for a scheduled interview in 1977 or 1978 with then-governor David Pryor, provided Cunningham with a sharp reminder of the Hill he'd first encountered as a job applicant. Cunningham's recollections, forty-plus years later, remained vivid:

On the appointed day, we set out in my 1973 MG GT hatchback, rather new at that time with likely less than 20,000 miles on it. Along the way, we heard a "pop" coming from under the hood. What happened next, I think, gives insight into Jack's personality. I pulled over, raised the hood, and discovered we had a broken fan belt. Jack remained in the passenger seat. Of course there were no portable phones in those days, so I tried to think about our options. Jack remained in the passenger seat. Finally, I decided we could drive a short distance until the motor got hot, then stop and cool it, then go again until we reached an exit. This worked, stopping three or four times. At the first exit, we miraculously found an auto repair shop with a fan belt to fit this fairly exotic car. We exceeded the speed limit on to Little Rock, pulling into the KATV parking lot just as the Governor's entourage arrived in his limo. As we were getting "miked" for the interview, I remember the Governor saying, "You guys look so serious, smile a little." Little did he know! Throughout this stressful time Jack sat in the passenger seat, offering no commiseration or suggestions, almost as if ignoring the problem. I can't imagine anyone else I know reacting in this way.[23]

The Pryor interview was conducted by both Cunningham and Hill and focused on topics of particular interest to KAIT's audience, but just a year or two later, in January of 1979, Hill was on his own in another Little Rock interview with Hillary Rodham, then in her first month as Arkansas's First Lady. The travel misadventures of the earlier session find their parallel here in the obvious unease of the interviewer contrasted to the blithe composure of the interviewee. Ms. Rodham's unprecedented youth (she's thirty-one), her appearance at the studio with no makeup and thick glasses, the fact that she'd kept her own name and was continuing as the governor's wife to practice law in Little Rock—all this Hill finds discomfiting. He apparently assumes viewers will share his bewilderment, since questions about her name and continuing work dominate the first half of the twenty-eight-minute interview, at times rephrased as follow-up queries to Rodham's initial replies, as if the interviewer is having difficulty wrapping his head around what he's hearing. Rodham, meanwhile, serenely knocks everything out, displaying at no time the slightest awareness of anything remotely controversial in her views or behavior.[24]

Hill's opening is an especially clumsy moment—he begins the interview by asking for the new First Lady's sense of her position's role, "if it can be called a position." Rodham doesn't miss a beat. "I think it is a position," she replies before moving smoothly to a presentation of her views and plans. A subsequent question, equally flat-footed, focuses on Rodham's apparent lack of interest in "state dinners, teas, and garden parties," offered as activities "we tend to associate with governors' wives." She swats this one too, with not a syllable in dispraise of state dinners or garden parties (she sends them back as "civic events and social events"). "I'm interested in everything," she says. The matter of her keeping her own name is also handled with breezy dispatch. Before she married Bill Clinton, she notes, she'd already developed a career as a law professor and practicing attorney as Hillary Rodham. A professional woman keeping her own name is nothing to raise eyebrows—"Anita

Bryant didn't take her husband's name," she adds in passing.[25]

It all comes across even now as a winning, bravura performance. Rodham simply dazzled Hill. The newsman's report to his wife that evening was couched in superlatives—he was shocked by the glasses and lack of cosmetics, he told Anne. "'But then,' he continued, 'she opened her mouth, and I totally forgot the way she looked, I was so taken aback by her intelligence and her ability to articulate.'" An auditor poised for offense could easily go ballistic here—another bozo Y chromosome meeting a young woman and anticipating an airhead. This would be a great overreaction. In the first place, Hill is on all occasions a stiffly formal presence, something of a klutz in any interview. He had in addition an exaggerated respect for educational achievement. In his introductory remarks, he'd listed Rodham's undergraduate degree from Wellesley and her law degree from Yale. Hill was also no stranger to working with professional women—at the time of the interview with Rodham, he was sharing KAIT's anchor desk with Becky Allison. His high praise for Rodham's poise and articulateness is thus best understood as made by a seasoned journalist with interviews with the likes of J. William Fulbright and David Pryor under his belt. He was still blown away and, by his wife's later report, spent the rest of his life convinced Rodham was the alpha brain of the Clinton team.[26]

By this time, Hernreich's upgrade program was in full gear. By 1981 the news division at KAIT would have a staff of eighteen. Hill had been promoted to public affairs director, and since 1978 he'd shared the news anchor desk with Allison. "I arrived the same month as videotape," Allison recalled. "November 4, 1978. By the time I got there, Jack had nothing to do with the day-to-day except to anchor. Cal [Wasson] was the news director. Jack read the news at noon, six, and ten, and he kind of did whatever he wanted with the documentaries. That was Jack's gig."[27]

"And Then They Sold the Station"

By 1978 Hill was no longer the newcomer just out of graduate school who struggled in Denver and Dallas with superiors who doubted him and chaffed in Jackson at the station's management policies and resistance to socially progressive reporting. He was well into his third year in Jonesboro, successful at both the anchor desk and in the developing field of news video programming. He turned thirty-eight the May before Allison arrived in November—not yet a grizzled veteran but certainly a seasoned professional who anchored a top-rated news desk and had collected a full shelf of regional and national awards. "Channel 8 is a small station in a university town," Allison recalled, "so they hired lots of young people. Arkansas State University had a very good reputation in their radio-TV department. It was a beginning place for people who wanted to try to make it in TV news."[28] In retrospect, George Hernreich's decision to open a television station in Jonesboro appears remarkably savvy. He had ripe for the taking a large underserved if widely dispersed market audience, plus a local university's already strong journalism department ahead of the curve in its broadcast offerings. In Darrel Cunningham he'd located an innovative and energetic station manager who in turn recognized a Dallas cab driver's potential and surrounded him with a strong news desk team and a skilled cameraman who worked well with his strengths and covered his weaknesses. By 1977, three years into Hill's tenure, they were off and running with their first award-winning special programs, and by 1985, nearing the end of a decade at the station, Hill had a stellar list of awards and was the face of a proven broadcast institution, dominant in its market and respected coast-to-coast.

In this workplace Hill, Wood, and Clay stood out as old hands. "Jack was the solemn, well-educated, above-the-fray guy," Allison remembered. "I'm sure he felt like he was stuck in broadcast day care with all these young twentysomethings. But he was doing what he wanted to do. He was winning awards for the station. It was a marvelous agreement. And then they sold the station."[29]

They did. On July 9, 1984, Hernreich sold KAIT to Nashville-based Channel Communications. "George Hernreich decided to take the money out," Cunningham recalled. "We had built it into a pretty well-respected community institution. We're making money, and it's turned into a pretty valuable property. So George, as was his right, decides it's time to harvest. He'd put a lot of money into it over the years, and he had a right to a good retirement."[30]

Things changed immediately and not for the better. Station manager Cunningham was initially asked to stay on, but nothing in his prior experience prepared him for the new environment:

> I'd only worked for this family-owned operation where I could talk with the principals and influence them. . . . So it was a good relationship, and

if we wanted to do something that was going to aggravate the local power structure, they didn't complain. They left it to us. And during all this time, this ten-year period, while Jack is doing his pieces, sometimes controversial pieces, Jack is writing the copy, and I'm going over it with him. He's gotta get it past me—I'm the gatekeeper. We do not have an attorney on staff. . . .

So we got this new corporation, and they've got a guy. He's in Nashville, and he wants everything we're gonna do that has any whiff of controversy to come through him first. . . . And Jack became immediately frustrated with this, and so did I.[31]

Cunningham left first, fired in early 1985, according to his account, while Hill resigned immediately on July 23 when new manager Bill McDonald demanded he sign an agreement taking him off all investigative stories in St. Francis County. It was a sudden, devastating end to what had been a glorious decade-long run. Recognizing its demoralizing impact, the Hills' pastor spent that night at the now-jobless anchorman's home.

Even as the awards and ratings successes had brought reassuring proof of his journalistic abilities, the day-to-day life behind these successes had afforded Hill and his wife a newfound financial security and sense of community standing. As Anne remembered it: "We bought the house on Merrill Cove while it was under construction and enjoyed the years we had there. . . . Jack enjoyed working in the yard. He had grown up mowing lawns. He insisted on buying a push mower that would not wake up all the neighbors. It was hard even then to find a push mower. He had to special order it from Sears. One day he was out mowing, and neighbor children came up and watched him in wonder. They asked, 'Mr. Hill, is that some new kind of lawn mower?'"[32]

But then, with the sharp finality of a contract no vertebrate journalist could sign, it all came to a crashing end. It took some time for the full impact to register. Hill had been down before, before Cunningham and KAIT had rescued him from Dallas, but now he had a solid decade's anchor-desk work on his resume, plus the major awards for his investigative programs. Surely there would be new opportunities, other stations in other towns eager for his services. He'd been a star, the face of broadcast news in Jonesboro and Northeast Arkansas. Bigger markets, cities with multiple broadcast outlets, were close by on every side. Little Rock? Memphis? Springfield? Perhaps it was time to move up?

Offers from such outlets would never materialize, though the couple had no way of knowing this at the time. Nineteen seventy-five to 1985 at KAIT, Anne's banking job, the church, their own house and yard and money in the bank—rebuilding this cozy world would prove elusive. A long-term perspective is poor solace for people facing present dangers, but the sudden end of the Jonesboro run may be less surprising when viewed in the light of industry-wide developments. At the beginning, Hill had been fortunate. His time as a journalism graduate student at Missouri had positioned him perfectly to be a pioneering analyst of network television's emergence as a primary news source for an overseas military conflict. Here he arrived at the beginning, with fellowship aid and departmental faculty guidance providing the institutional support required for sustained analysis. Twenty years later he was in nearly the exact opposite position, placed squarely in the crosshairs in the early years of take-overs of local broadcast stations and newspapers by communications conglomerates with absentee ownerships. This time he was present, as a target, at the beginning of the end. The 1984 sale was only the first—just two years later the station changed hands again, sold this time to Cosmos Broadcasting, itself a subsidiary of Liberty Corporation. The gobbling continues to this day—Raycom Media bought KAIT in 2006, and 2019 saw it sold again, acquired by Gray Television.

None of these moves returned ownership to Jonesboro or to Arkansas. Hill's days as a local Walter Cronkite, measured and reserved in manner, projecting a fair-minded respect for both his material and his audience, gave way to a very different model. Lines separating news and entertainment blurred at the expense of the former, enlarging the latter in a fast-paced spectacle. News anchors, especially at the local level, morphed nearly overnight into Kens and Barbies, feathers primped and smoothed by hairdressers and wardrobe managers, mouthing scripts prepared and vetted by others. There they are, every day, earnestly enthusiastic about ex-celebrity dance-athons and on-screen marriage proposals, hawking their bosses' programming wares and political slants. Less bread with extra helpings of circus. The weather folks, forever forecasting disaster, are now heavier presences. This was the coming world in 1985, and Jack Hill, sober, serious, unswervingly earnest, was suddenly old and in the way. (If this summary comes off as flippant overstatement, here's the same point expressed in more restrained language, made by a fellow journalist: "Those who read the news are usually promoted as 'celebrities,' rather than journalists.")[33]

For both cultural moments—the televised war and the ongoing corporate take-overs of broadcast stations—Hill was present at the beginning, fortunate as a pioneering analyst for the first, an early casualty of the second. From a closer-to-the-ground vantage point, however, there was little new in any of it. Hill and KAIT didn't require corporate take-overs for their investigative efforts to offend exposed slumlords, on-the-job drunks, and sheriffs on the take. Shortly after coming on board as station manager, Cunningham "somehow wangled an invitation" to join an early-morning group of local movers and shakers who met weekly for breakfast and coffee. "There was a banker or two, a couple of lawyers," he remembered. "One of the group was this local judge—I think he was a municipal judge or circuit judge; I can't recall." When *Is There Any Hope for Hope Street?* aired in 1977, Cunningham found his seat at the table had heated up: "One of the major property owners in this area was this judge. And Jack named his name, showed the poor conditions of the property along with interviews from tenants saying they couldn't get stuff fixed or repaired. And of course the judge was highly irate. You can imagine what he had to say to me when I showed up at the coffee klatch! It was funny in a way but testy in a way. We certainly were not going to pull any punches. We weren't going to back off because he was part of the local power structure."[34]

The new owners had a very different approach, as Cunningham and Hill learned to their dismay: "This is a corporate ownership. Their only interest is making money. They don't care whether the residents of Hope Street need help. They don't care whether the water table in eastern Arkansas is lowering and is going to affect everybody's life in the coming decades. They don't care. They care about money, period. . . . They were not interested in doing anything that was controversial."[35]

Other area journalists were not slow to notice events in Jonesboro, and one at least was quick to go public with his tart response. Roy Ockert Jr. was editor of neighboring Independence County's *Batesville Daily Guard* when his fellow journalist resigned after being "called off the St. Francis County story to 'redirect his general journalistic concepts.'" Just over a week later, on August 1, Ockert devoted his Behind the News op-ed piece to incisive critique. "TV Station Takes Ax to Coverage" was his frontal-assault headline, and though he quoted station manager McDonald's positive spin—"We're not going to de-emphasize Batesville or anywhere else"—Ockert noted in his lead that the station had both dismissed the only reporter assigned to North Arkansas and "forced the resignation of its award-winning newscaster, Jack Hill." He went on to remind the new owners that the station not only served "more than 300,000 homes in 33 Northeast Arkansas counties" but "more importantly, has won the confidence of its viewers." Ockert concluded his evisceration by calling the retreat from the St. Francis County story "a black mark on journalism and a disgrace to the news director who made the decision."[36]

Ockert was right on in his critique, but of course his defense of journalistic practice and his now-unemployed colleague had exactly zero discernible effect. He, like Hill and Cunningham and Allison and Scales and their occupational colleagues everywhere, was up against tectonic shifts in communications technologies and corporate restructurings. Ockert would himself soon leave Batesville to become editor of the *Jonesboro Sun*, while Cunningham would move to Fort Smith, still working for the Hernreichs at their linked Fort Smith and Fayetteville stations, KHBS/KHOG.

Coolidge Conlee and Wayne DuMond

For Jack and Anne Hill, the landing would be harder. Close attention to the dates makes clear that Hill was already jobless when he flew off to 1986 IRE conventions in San Antonio and Portland to serve on panels and accept awards for the *I Run This County* series. These conventions occurred in June (Portland) and October (San Antonio), just before and just after the one-year anniversary of his resignation and only months after Sheriff Conlee had filed his $7.5 million suit against the award-winning panelist. It must have been a downright disorienting experience—on the one hand, folks are handing you plaques and colleagues eager to replicate your successes are taking notes at your panel presentations. Applause wells up. Meanwhile, back home, court dates loom. You've got lawyers to pay and no checks coming in. "Not many people want to hire a reporter with a pending $7.5 million lawsuit," Anne Hill told a reporter for a story published two days after Conlee's indictment in 1988, "even one with Jack's credentials. . . . The last three years have been hard on us." For his part, Hill told the same reporter, "It's been an ordeal, a nightmare. . . . You begin to think, 'Have I sacrificed my career for this.'"[37]

Conlee's indictment ended his lawsuit's threat, but other facets of the story were already developing in ways that added to Hill's frustrations. His initial

Conlee investigations, focused on the sheriff's central role in bootlegging and gambling operations in St. Francis County and suspicious circumstances surrounding a fire that destroyed his crop-dusting business, had aired on nightly newscasts through the week beginning Monday, February 11, 1985, and closed with the half-hour *I Run This County* special program on Sunday the seventeenth. Just eighteen days later, Sheriff Conlee had become a central player in a story far more lurid and longer running than arson or bootlegging and gambling activities.

On March 7, Wayne DuMond, a thirty-five-year-old laborer awaiting trial for the rape of a Forrest City high school girl the previous September, was by his own report castrated by two masked men who broke into his home while he was watching television. Sheriff Conlee arrived belatedly at the scene but eventually left after taking possession of the severed testicles (he labeled them evidence)—by one account carried in a matchbox from DuMond's residence to a local funeral home operated by the county coroner, who also happened to also be the father of the rape victim.

A story ending here would already come across as a laughably overblown B-movie script, but Conlee was just getting started. Placed in a jar and immersed in formaldehyde, DuMond's gonads ended up on the sheriff's office desk, exhibited to colleagues and favored visitors. One of these reported Conlee as telling him "this was what happened if you raped the wrong girl in his county" (the victim was a distant cousin of then-governor Bill Clinton).[38] Tabloids raced to Arkansas for the story, and as it turned out, the public career of DuMond's testicles provoked an interest comparable to that provoked by the earlier castration. Speedily convicted on the rape charge and collared with a life-plus-twenty sentence, he was shipped south to Cummins prison farm.

Conlee drove the escort car to the penitentiary, but his triumph was short lived. The locked-up inmate now presenting as victim (his testicles had in the interim apparently been flushed down a toilet) had little difficulty successfully prosecuting a civil suit against the sheriff. A "tort of outrage" filed on his behalf, followed by a trial in US District Court in August of 1988, resulted in a judgment against Conlee of $50,000 in punitive damages and $100,000 in compensatory damages. Not even a convicted and castrated rapist, the jury concluded, deserved such public humiliation. Conlee's public exhibition of DuMond's privates constituted an egregious and arbitrary invasion, an "inhumane abuse of official power literally shocking to the conscience."[39]

The entire investigation of the castration (and the preceding rape) was bungled from the beginning at forensic and judicial levels, leading to a decades-long saga of appeals and parole board hearings tarring two Arkansas governors and presidential candidates (Clinton and Mike Huckabee). A network television show (ABC's *20/20* in 1989) and a New York tabloid news and culture journal (the *Village Voice* in 2001) took the story to the nation. Sheriff Conlee's bizarre behavior in the immediate aftermath of the castration was itself headline grabbing, and Hill's dogged pursuit would soon drag him into the DuMond case. The linked Conlee and DuMond stories would dominate Hill's personal and professional life for the rest of the decade.

On the surface, his two subjects could hardly have been more different. The lawman, despite his wiry, bantamweight build, was a swaggering, larger-than-life character at the center of the region's mainstream life—prior to his multiterm run as St. Francis County sheriff, he'd served a stint as mayor of Forrest City. "I run this county," he said. The accused rapist was by all appearances a polar opposite, a nobody who ran nothing, an odd-jobs laborer with a long trail of near-miss escapes from prosecution for sexual and homicidal violence in his wake. Both men were bad actors, as it turned out, their bottom-level similarities eclipsing the surface differences, but Hill ended up spending the better part of six years pursuing their intertwined stories, a recognized adversary of the sheriff and a no less high-profile advocate for the prisoner. When the dust settled, Hill would be one for two, right on every count about the lawman, just as deeply wrong about the inmate.

Convinced that Conlee was guilty of a spectacular range of criminal operations, Hill pursued him tenaciously in the teeth of every obstacle. The sheriff eventually went down, owing in large part to the now-jobless journalist's reporting, in a textbook instance of the profession discharging its fourth-estate responsibilities as a guardian of the public weal. Little in the way of perceptible blowback occurred—Hill took all his heat on the front end, most of it from Conlee himself and the employers who cut him off at both microphone and wallet. At the episode's close, if still out of a steady job, he found himself lauded again, this time in the in-state press, for the same persistent work that had garnered awards in the first half of the decade. An *Arkansas Democrat* editorial published shortly after Conlee's indictment wondered in print if justice might also be in the offing for the reporter whose "freelance investigative pieces" played a crucial role in ending Conlee's "reign as exalted high sheriff over the St Francis political machine." "But how about former Jonesboro television anchorman Jack E. Hill," the column asked, "who's still paying the price of steady unemployment for, of all things, dedicated investigative reporting?"[40] Not only is "steady unemployment" a striking phrasal gem, but the whole long story, loaded with ups and downs, ends in straightforward closure, with Conlee locked up and Hill secure in victory and virtue's camp.

No less convinced that the case against DuMond was deeply flawed, compromised by police and judicial incompetence mixed with external political pressures, Hill worked with matching industry to assist the convict who seemed to him locked away without the benefit of anything resembling due process. Whole boxes of court documents and newspaper clippings tracking DuMond's trial and appeals are preserved in Hill's papers, along with several letters to the Hills from DuMond's wife. Gradually, both husband and wife found themselves swallowed up in the case—Anne Hill ended up working part-time on the case in the offices of attorney John Wesley Hall Jr., who was handling the civil suit against Conlee. Guy Reel's book-length account of the case mentions a 1987 visit to the Hills' home by DuMond's wife and children.[41]

The result this time was strikingly different. Where Conlee went to jail and stayed, DuMond eventually went free, paroled in 1997 (though not actually let out until 1999) at the urging of then-governor and future-presidential-candidate Huckabee. Hill's efforts, again, had played a prominent role. It didn't take the parolee long to prove his release a grave mistake—in June of 2001, Missouri authorities using

DNA evidence charged him with a rape and murder committed the previous fall, only six weeks after he'd moved to the Kansas City area. Convicted in 2003, DuMond was facing charges in a second rape and murder (this one from 2001) when he died in his Missouri prison cell in 2005.

For Hill, the whole drawn-out saga conspicuously lacked the Conlee story's secure niche in right livelihood. DuMond, as Hill was convinced, may have gone in shackles to Cummins on less-than-solid legal grounds, but in hindsight's sharper light, it is obvious that efforts devoted to his release were tragically misdirected. If you're one of the folks—and there were many—who in service to whatever mix of self-serving and high-minded motives turned DuMond loose, you're ever after lugging around heavy loads of second guesses. People died when he went free.

Scraping By

As both the Conlee and DuMond stories dragged through the papers and courts, Jack and Anne Hill struggled to keep their lives together at the most basic level. They faced a very tough climb, as Anne, despite having won job performance awards earlier, had lost her banking job just months before her husband was presented with his unsignable contract. The welcome mat in Jonesboro had been suddenly withdrawn, and they once again had to scramble, as Hill had done before in Denver and husband and wife had done together as newlyweds in Dallas. The house with the vintage lawn mower was sold, and when the proceeds ran out, they cashed in their IRAs.

Meanwhile, through it all, the journalist without a desk kept working. Within four months of the KAIT resignation, Hill had reached an agreement with John Robert Starr, managing editor at the *Arkansas Democrat*, "to collect information and to produce news articles on the political situation in St. Francis County."[42] For this work Hill received $5,000 in five installments, beginning with a first payment on December 1, 1985, and ending with a final installment on February 1, 1986. He also got reimbursement for travel and meal expenses, with Starr thus explicitly assigning, and paying for, the very work expressly forbidden by the professional neutering offered by the Channel Communications contract at KAIT. Hill must have savored the connection as a bittersweet triumph.

The *Democrat* work resulted in a "St. Francis Machine" series, several of its installments written or co-authored with staffer Jan Meins, which ran over a nearly two-month span in the spring of 1986. These pieces caused quite a stir—Conlee blamed them for his defeat in the following fall's primary elections. The Hills, feeling run out of Jonesboro, had by this time moved to Little Rock in search of higher-than-zero employment opportunities. Anne Hill gradually moved from banking into working in law offices following her stints working on the DuMond case for John Wesley Hall. For his part, Hill followed up his work for the *Democrat* with an assignment in Fort Smith, where Darrel Cunningham came through with a job at the linked KHBS/KHOG stations. Here the two produced in 1989 another prize-winning program developed via their old KAIT model of a week of shorter presentations edited into a half-hour special. This one was an investigation of illegal cockfighting rings in Arkansas and eastern Oklahoma, complete with hidden-camera video. The old Cunningham-Hill magic held again—*Cockfighting* collected the 1990 regional award for investigative reporting at the Radio-Television News Directors Association meeting in San Jose, California. The winners, according to an article in *Electronic Media*, the trade journal that covered the convention, "set themselves apart from the pack by taking risks that resulted in outstanding investigative reports."[43]

Both the *Democrat* and KHBS jobs, welcome as they must have been, were stopgaps, significant financial and professional boosts but no substitute for regular, full-time employment. For the last half of the 1980s at least, money was always either running out or already gone. Hill never drove a cab again, but at one low point, he took a job in telemarket-ing (selling newspaper subscriptions, of all things). "At the worst," Anne Hill remembered, "Jack went to give blood at a plasma center where they gave you $15, and I tried to hock my aunt's pearls that I had inherited, only to find out they were fake! . . . We led a hand-to-mouth existence."[44] A later reminis-cence resurrected a still more desperate moment: "Whenever things would get really bad, I would call Jack's parents and ask for help. When we were living in Little Rock and things were at their worst, they paid our apartment rent for a while."[45]

As he had in the early 1970s in Dallas, Hill would sometimes despair not only of his place in the world of journalism but also of journalism itself as a distinguished profession with an essential watch-dog role in civil life. This note is clear in the unpub-lished "Unequal Justice Under the Law," where Hill's detailed account of his efforts to find editors willing to support and publish his DuMond research ends in defeat. "It was a numbing experience," he writes. "I succeeded seven times in obtaining a hearing with editors and managers of news organizations serving Arkansas. The effort seemed wasted." The lengthy essay ends, after moving from the grim Arkansas story to wide-ranging allusions to events from the First and Second World Wars and "the job the Founding Fathers expected," with dire if clichéd warnings: "The decisive battles won't involve a foreign threat. The real battles are here at home—in the choices we make."[46]

This bromide may hold a truth at its center, but in the instance under review, it surely doesn't help that Hill turned out to be spectacularly wrong—he was laboring diligently on behalf of a man whose entry in Arkansas's standard online reference source describes him in its opening sentence as "a serial rapist and killer."[47] "Unequal Justice Under the Law" is a dark-minded piece from start to finish, a peevish, even petulant screed written in defiant exasperation by a once-lionized journalist subjected to nearly half a decade's professional ostracism and financial desperation even as his work was applauded.

Eighteen months earlier, Hill had issued a much briefer lecture on journalism's civic responsibilities. Unlike the essay, this profile/interview was published, appearing under a "Whatever Happened to Jack Hill" headline in the *Northeast Arkansas Town Crier*, a weekly newspaper published in Manila, Arkansas. A good bit of it might be read as "Unequal Justice Under the Law" compressed to abstract. The central watchdog duties of a free press are again proclaimed: "If the people are not informed, how in the world can they make decisions of importance." The price paid by the Hills for their commitment to these duties is once more cited: "My wife has received threatening phone calls, I have been beaten on camera, our car has been spray painted, and I have been alienated from my profession." The refusal of Arkansas media outlets to publish the full range of his research on the DuMond story is lamented: "I have had the support of some of the people in my profession, but not the profession itself."[48]

This same piece, however, for all its brevity, also contains two items of very different tone. One describes a specific recent accomplishment, while the other puts forward a general plan for the future. The accomplishment was a one-hour special program devoted to former Arkansas senator J. William Fulbright, which had aired "last December" (in 1986, linked to Arkansas's sesquicentennial celebrations). Hill is listed as "reporter-producer," and the program, titled *Fulbright*, is described as a "joint venture between the television station KTHV of Little Rock and the Winthrop Rockefeller Foundation." The general plan was for more of the same: "I am working on proposals now," Hill said, "for educational t.v. in the hopes of airing an hourly show, similar to *60 Minutes*, that will deal with the people of Arkansas."[49]

Fulbright, airing in 1986, was both something wholly familiar and something promisingly new. Hill had worked as "reporter-producer" on more than a dozen such special reports during his time at KAIT. He was an old hand at putting such programs together, building them up from a week's worth of shorter segments. *Fulbright*, at nearly an hour's length, was twice the length of the KAIT specials, but that wasn't the truly new element. Every KAIT special program had been the work of a team of employees working within the station's institutional structure, supported by regular paychecks and an allocated budget. With *Fulbright*, Hill was working not as an employee of KTHV but as a freelance pioneer of documentary film journalism in Arkansas. One year later, in 1987, he would be billed as "Reporter/Producer" for another hour-long special, *Health Care: The Crisis in Arkansas*, funded by the same sponsors. The credits, dated August 28, 1987, list this piece as produced by the Arkansas Television Company, the corporate entity operating KHTV; directed by Steve Doan, who was then the station's production manager; and shot by cameraman Dale Carpenter, then working at the Arkansas Educational Television Network.

The work with Carpenter ended up inaugurating a durable and fruitful collaboration, as Carpenter remembers:

> I did that work for Jack as a freelance videographer. I had previously been a news photographer/editor at KATV 7 but not for KTHV 11. I remember being introduced to Jack at a party in Little Rock when he first told me about his idea for TeleVision for Arkansas. He had seen some of my AETN films and was looking for a shooter. My plate was full, but since he was going to produce, write, and edit the films, I agreed to shoot them for him on a per-day basis. It was a good opportunity for me to earn some extra money.
>
> I soon found out that Jack would always get his money's worth. The days were tightly scheduled, packed from morning to night. We would shoot a thirty-minute film in three days that usually stretched into fourteen-to-sixteen-hour marathons. As a producer for AETN, I was used to having months to shoot a documentary with unlimited use of the cameras. Jack rented his

camera by the day, so we would usually pick up the gear the day before his rental period began and shoot something that evening, followed by another long day. I had to work very fast. I looked at shooting with Jack as an exercise in how to shoot quickly and maintain quality. And I always felt like the stories he was telling were worth doing.

The Arkansas Television Company, then, was not Jack Hill's company, but over a two-year span, he'd been centrally involved in the making of two hour-long films, the primary on-camera interviewer on both. Just over two years later, in October 1989, TeleVision for Arkansas released its first film. As with the earlier films, Hill was the interviewer, the reporter, the producer. But now he was also the owner, running his own show, working with a trusted cameraman whose endurance matched his own. Over the next decade or so, the Hill-Carpenter team would work together on some forty films.

It was a long, difficult, and often deeply depressing struggle after KAIT's new owners cut Hill loose in 1985, a five-to-six-year stretch before he was able to establish anything like a steady routine and reopen an even semireliable revenue stream. But if *Fulbright*, appearing a year and a half after the axe fell, stands out in retrospect as a first harbinger of a better future, the "proposals now for educational t.v." aimed at "the people of Arkansas" might be understood as auguring that future's imminent arrival. As the 1980s ended, the decade's second half as difficult as the first had been successful, there would be more such proposals, addressed to a wide range of public and private sponsors and granting agencies, and their eventual success would at last open a path to the applicant's most enduring work. The hoped-for "hourly show" never materialized, but Jack Hill, drummed out of the broadcast journalism world where he'd won his highest honors, was gradually reinventing himself as a pioneer Arkansas documentary filmmaker.

CHAPTER 3

HISTORIAN WITH A CAMERA

From Employee to Entrepreneur

The hints of a promising future offered up to the modest readership of the *Northeast Arkansas Town Crier* in 1987 found their first sustained realization in the early 1990s. In the first five years of the decade, Hill produced twenty films for broadcast on various commercial stations, picking up the pace with each passing year. *The Way Out*, the earliest title issued by TeleVision for Arkansas, Hill's newly established independent production company, appeared at the end of 1989 (in October), followed by *Two Families* in 1990. Both were Arkansas success stories rooted in determined pursuit of higher education. *The Way Out* focused on three University of Arkansas football stars, while *Two Families* opened with the story of Major League Baseball star Wally Moon, whose family insisted that college precede his professional career. (Moon had a master's degree in hand before his rookie season with the St. Louis Cardinals in 1954.) Even this level of commitment paled next to that demonstrated by the saga of the second family— Ethel and Julius Kearney were poor southeastern Arkansas sharecroppers, but they were so insistent on education that eighteen of their nineteen children obtained college degrees and several went on to distinguished careers as attorneys and educators. Hill was by this time living in Little Rock, but for his initial efforts, he relied most on the eastern sections of the state he knew best from his news desk work—the football stars of *The Way Out* were from Marianna in Lee County, the Moons hailed from Bay in Craighead County, and the Kearneys farmed near Gould in Lincoln County.

Hill broadened his geographical range for a second 1990 production—*Back to School* was another celebration of education's value, but it followed the efforts of three adults returning to college in Bentonville, Pine Bluff, and Arkadelphia. Here, in only his third independent film, aired one year after his first, he clearly intended to make good the claim of his company's name. He would produce television for Arkansas, all of Arkansas. Hill doubled his list of completed titles in 1991, with *Courage*, portraits of Arkansans learning to read in adult education programs; *Friday Night Heroes*, which despite the sports reference of the title, is another piece on the importance of education; and *Yes, I Can!*, a portrayal of three single mothers who pursue higher education as a path to better futures for themselves and their children. In just over a two-year period at the outset of his career as an independent producer, Hill thus completed and arranged airtime for six films celebrating educational efforts in every section of Arkansas at every level from ABCs to graduate school. He wasn't his school principal mother, but he was following closely in her footsteps.

This is a very high, even astonishing level of productivity, clearly rooted in his news background—

many documentary filmmakers are more than happy to complete a single film in a year's work. Les Blank, among the nation's best-known documentary filmmakers, lived through almost the same period as Hill (born five years earlier, in 1935, Blank died a year later, in 2013). Blank's company, Flower Films, issued its first title in 1968; he codirected his final film in 2007. His filmography lists forty-one titles over forty-five years, many of them big award winners of much greater length and broader scope than anything Hill produced. Michael Moore is still better known, though not so universally lauded. He made *Roger and Me*, his first film, in 1989. *Bowling for Columbine* won an Academy Award, and *Fahrenheit 9/11* broke box-office earning records for American documentaries. He's still working. IMDb credits him with twenty-two films over twenty-nine years, many of them blockbusters.

These comparisons are at most levels fanciful. Blank is renowned among filmmakers, and Moore, the documentary gadfly, has been listed as one of the world's top hundred wielders of influence, however that might be measured. Jack Hill didn't breathe these rare airs. He wasn't Ken Burns. His sights were set on state-level goals, and while reinventing himself as a documentary filmmaker, he never really deviated from the newsman's fundamental devotion to informational, get-the-story priorities. The pictures, even in his chosen visual medium, never trump the words. As cameraman Carpenter puts it, "Jack rarely paused in his films to let the visuals and natural sounds speak for themselves. There is usually someone talking throughout. And he was averse to using music, unless it was from scenes we shot for the film, such as the fife and drum music in *War in the '60s.*" Hill's surviving papers preserve scores of scripts for the audio track of this or that project, with analogously detailed shot lists for the video sequences nowhere to be found. But in sheer productivity, in speedily turning out his work and getting it to Arkansas television screens, he had no peer.

He only upped the ante in 1992, completing four new films. *Freedom* was a follow-up to the previous year's *Courage*, checking on the reading progress of the adult learners, while *Red Bugs and Scholarships*, celebrating the athletic and academic successes of Fordyce high school students, was a revisiting of the themes of *Friday Night Heroes*. There was also a perceptible expansion of thematic range—*Born Too Small*, focused on the special needs and services available to families with low-birth-weight infants, was the first Hill film not centrally focused on educational issues. More would follow. *War Comes to Arkansas* was another first, Hill's initial effort at a televised presentation of Arkansas's Civil War history. After 1992, the steady increase in productivity continued—TeleVision for Arkansas produced five films in 1993 and six in 1994.

Hill's work from the beginning thus centered on a sharply focused list of subject areas that would occupy him for the rest of his career: Educational and public health issues would hold the early top spots, with significant episodes in Arkansas history (especially military history) moving to the lead in later efforts. Sports would also be in the mix from the start, and a combined focus on athletics and education, leading with the former to introduce a more sustained attention to the latter, would quickly emerge as something of a signature narrative strategy. *Red Bugs and Scholarships* opens and closes with scenes from Fordyce football games, but its central focus is the impressive support provided for college costs to approximately half the local high school graduates by a locally established and administered scholarship association. Produced at KHBS in Fort Smith with credits to seven local and state-level sponsors, it aired in January of 1992 on KLRT in Little Rock. Yet another effort in this vein was *A Triplet Returns*, from 1993, chronicling Razorback and NBA basketball star Ron Brewer's return to campus.

One especially compelling film from this period, certainly Hill's best overall achievement before *Arkansas' Black Gold* in 1996, is the 1994 *Work Will Win*, an account of the Fargo Agricultural School (FAS) operated for the education of African American children from 1920 to 1949 by Mississippi native Floyd Brown and his Arkansas-born wife, Lillie Epps Brown. Hill's title is strikingly uninformative—he took it from the school's motto—but the film itself offers a moving tribute to a pioneer Arkansas educator. Hill had been conspicuous at least since the days of the traffic congestion study for WFAA in Dallas and the housing reports in Jackson and Jonesboro for his attention to the lives of often neglected people, but *Work Will Win* shows the newsman turned filmmaker bringing similar perspectives to a history-based topic.

If the combination of sports and education would be a regular feature of Hill's efforts, the focus in *Red Bugs and Scholarships* on the single community of Fordyce would be unusual. From the start, as in his first celebrations of education's value, Hill cast a statewide net. Segments shot on multiple locations throughout the state would be a persistent feature of his productions, continuing to make good on the promise of his company's name. *Born Too Small* is typical in this regard, combining scenes from Blytheville, Little Rock, and Hot Springs. *Children of Hunger*, addressed to issues of child nutrition, moves from opening sequences on school-based programs in Arkadelphia to home visits in Miller County and a kindergarten breakfast program at Fayetteville's Leverett Elementary.

It wasn't long, either, before Hill developed the structural template he would deploy with minimal variation in film after film. The open is a short teaser, its audio providing date, place, and sometimes time of day for an on-location scene, followed by a stand-up intro by the producer in standard news reporter positioning, outdoors, facing the camera, most often dressed in coat and tie. "I'm Jack Hill," he says, before heading directly to the introduction of his subject. Sponsor credits follow, read by another announcer, before Hill's voice returns as the film's narrator. A standard thirty-minute Hill production included three additional credit sequences, two as breaks in the narrative and one at the close. Hill's on-screen appearances after the introductory stand-up are few and brief—most often cutaway shots of interviewer listening attentively to interviewee. Then, at the end, framing the whole, the voice of the producer-director returns for the sign-off. "This is Jack Hill," he says, "reporting for Arkansas."

Effective fundraising was essential to the success of TeleVision for Arkansas, and Hill threw himself into it with something of the same energy and tenacity he'd devoted to investigative reporting as far back as his *Homes like These* and *I Run This County* days in Jackson and Jonesboro. The seven sponsor credits listed for *Red Bugs and Scholarships* make up a longer-than-average roster, but most titles list at least three or four. Anne Hill recalled the first years as a steep uphill climb on the financial front: "I suggested that he hire someone to be the person to contact potential sponsors because I knew that was not his strong point. Busy executives did not have the time to listen to Jack go on and on, and that was the only way Jack knew to do it."[1]

Hill eventually managed without the extra hire thanks to a big break that greatly aided subsequent fundraising efforts. Sometime around 1990, as Anne Hill remembered, "someone opened the door for him with Rob Walton at Walmart and Walmart became his main sponsor for maybe the first year or more. . . . Jack would pitch the idea to Rob Walton, and he would write the initial check for sponsorship, which was usually $5000. Jack would then solicit sponsors related to the particular topic. If it were a topic about health, he would go to Blue Cross Blue Shield."[2]

In fact, Walmart became Hill's "main sponsor" over a much more extended period—not only providing major support for both *Red Bugs and Scholarships* and *Born Too Small*, among other early TeleVision for Arkansas productions, but also continuing this support throughout the 1990s and well into the new millennium. Examples of films completed with primary support from Walmart include *Children of Hunger*, from 1996; *The Newest Arkansans*, from 1999; and *Wings of Honor*, from 2005.

There are remarkable similarities, then, between Darrel Cunningham's rescue of Hill from his taxi-driving days in Dallas in 1975 and Rob Walton's $5,000 seed grants of the early 1990s. Cunningham, weathering his young job applicant's socially inept Memphis-to-Jonesboro monologue and sensing the drive and intelligence beneath it, had obtained for

KAIT the decade-long services of a solid news desk anchor whose long-form investigative stories won the station a full trophy case of prestigious national and regional awards. Fifteen years later, Rob Walton's lifeline grants brought a happy end to Hill's five-year journalistic exile by somehow seeing through the neophyte freelancer's "on and on" to appreciate the vision behind it. Walmart's grants, like Cunningham's job offer, were game changers. The first got its beneficiary ten years of steady work and an impressive CV, a happy and fruitful decade. The Walton grants paid off with twice that, launching the novice filmmaker on a two-decade career lasting to the end of his days.

At the beginning, as the 1990s opened and Hill was just getting started with TeleVision for Arkansas, a $5,000 seed-money commitment from Walmart in hand, he could approach other potential donors with newfound confidence. If Rob Walton (he was director of what was then known as the Walton Family Charitable Support Foundation) was on board in support of one or another film project, surely others would be more inclined to appreciate its merits. They were, and by the middle of the decade, Hill was turning out as many as a half dozen films each year.

Like any new business, TeleVision for Arkansas at times produced work motivated wholly by economic motives. The paying customer is always at least partly right. Hill never entirely escaped the need for this kind of bill-paying work. As late as 2004, he was turning out *We're Taking Off*, a five-minute promo for the Lawrence County Chamber of Commerce. An earlier instance might be *Destination Arkansas*, a 1993 effort focused on campaigns to encourage trade associations, professional groups, and tourism operators to include Arkansas attractions and meeting facilities in their convention and vacation plans. The Little Rock Convention and Visitors Bureau and the Eureka Springs Chamber of Commerce, among others, joined with regular sponsors (Walmart, Electric Cooperatives of Arkansas) on this one. The 1995 *We're Number One!* would appear to be another do-it-for-the-money project. A fast-paced production, it touches down briefly at nearly twenty widespread points across the state to highlight world-leading business operations of various kinds. A cotton gin in Leachville, a wood processing plant in Crossett, a brickmaking facility in Malvern, a field of disease-resistant spinach in Alma, a rice mill in Stuttgart, bait-fish ponds in Lonoke and Prairie Counties—all these and more are celebrated. Southwestern Bell Telephone and Georgia-Pacific, among others, helped cover costs.

A certain level of pathos adheres from the start to such efforts—folks getting loud about being champs are on volume alone suspected of harboring doubt. And here's poor Hill, in his opening stand-up for *The Newest Arkansans* (one of his better films), earnestly assuring viewers that Arkansans "have lots of number ones—makes you wonder why we've had an inferiority complex all these years." Another low point shows up in the 2006 *Currents of History*, when a proud Lawrence County archivist exhibits a legal document signed by Stephen F. Austin. Following Hill's voice-over noting Austin's renown as "the Father of Texas," the archivist seals the claim: "For someone that famous to come through and to play a part in Arkansas history is really quite an exciting thing." Really? An out-of-state big-shot-to-be spends a single legislative session in town, signs a few autographs before leaving the building, and this is major news?

We're not number one, but number one slept here? Better, say most of Hill's films, we should be celebrating Floyd Brown, the students in Charleston, the hundreds of Arkansas Rosenwald Schools, the women and men who worked at the Civilian Conservation Corps camps and the Arkansas Ordnance Plant.

Such unalloyed booster moments are rare in TeleVision for Arkansas productions. If Hill sometimes shoots through rose-tinted lenses, he typically also insists on inclusion of somber shades. Celebrating in *New Schools for Arkansas* the life-changing contributions of the state's Rosenwald Schools in a time when "separate but equal" was the favored segregationist euphemism for public education policy, Hill first cites the bromide and then announces in stentorian, voice-from-the-heavens tones that separate as it certainly was, "it was not equal."

For the most part, even from the beginning, Hill was able to adroitly mix occupation and vocation, convince sponsors to support projects falling within subject areas already familiar from his prior work at KAIT and also dovetailing nicely with his own interests. From his days in Mississippi on, he'd been interested in social issues—in housing, in public health, in education, in matters of religious faith. Of these areas, only housing would drop off his screen as an independent filmmaker.

Another topic conspicuously absent from the new work was politics. He was as willing as ever to take on controversial issues—in 1994 he produced *My Brother's Keeper*, spotlighting the ravages of AIDS in Arkansas communities, where his open concern for and sympathy with its victims was a brave stance in a time of widespread public ostracism. But Hill the independent filmmaker was finished with slumlords and lawmen on the take. The years following his unhappy departure from KAIT in 1985 and from Jonesboro in 1986 had been hard in every way. Both Jack and Anne had lost jobs, and constant economic stresses had brought more fundamental personality differences to the surface. The wife of the teetotaler husband was drinking too much, and she resented her husband's mind-numbing monologues to party guests. "He wanted to be the talking person and for you to listen," Anne said in a 2016 interview. "I would see the look in their eyes—glazed. And I would go try to pull him off of them. Jack was a loner. He didn't need other people. I did." The couple separated in 1995 but didn't formally divorce until sixteen years later, in 2011. Their public behavior in the intervening period is a revealing tale unusual in reflecting credit to both parties. Anne's account fills in the story:

> I was the one who said, "Jack, this isn't working. It's my fault, but we need to end this."
>
> And he said, "Well, there's never been a divorce in our family. I don't want my mother to know about this." Well, she was on up in years by then, and his father had died, so he said, "All I know to do is just pretend we're still living together."
>
> So we would drive up there at Christmas and pretend like everything was fine, and we would sleep in the same room we had always slept in back when we were married, and we would get up and open the presents the next morning. His mother was the kind who always cooked the traditional Christmas dinner. It was bizarre.[3]

Bizarre, yes, but underneath the strangeness, rich in mutual consideration. Few sons are so devoted to their mothers, and not many ex-wives willingly devote fifteen Christmases to the unruffled happiness of an ex-mother-in-law. Few couples also divorce with such sustained reciprocal regard and concern for each other. When Anne's struggles with alcohol were at their most self-destructive, Jack arranged for an intervention and was her biggest sobriety cheerleader. At the end of his life, it was she who was still driving him to get prescriptions filled and calling to check on his condition.

The "loner" ex-husband, busy with his new filmmaking ventures, stayed alone—he'd meant it when he said "till death do us part," he told his ex-wife. As straitlaced to the end as he was from the beginning, ever the boy who insisted on being a Union soldier in neighborhood Civil War reenactments, Hill was sustained by a triple-barreled sense of mission at domestic, occupational, and spiritual levels. The most dutiful of sons and husbands, he conceived of journalism as a crucial component of social and political order and understood his Methodist faith as imparting a sense of divinely assigned mission to his work. Back in the earliest days of trouble in Jonesboro, when Jack's slum-housing piece was resented by local power brokers and Anne had asked him to pull back, he'd based his stubborn refusal on spiritual grounds. "And he said, 'I can't quit. I'm not a quitter. I think that God sent me to this earth to make a difference in people's lives,'" Anne recalled.[4]

Nearly a decade after Hill's death, the separate recollections of Anne Hill and Dale Carpenter lay stress on the continued bare-bones frugality of his later life by focusing on his car. Anne Hill remembered: "Jack had no money. . . . He drove a very old Buick with about two hundred thousand miles on it because that was all he could afford. Much of the money he inherited from his mother went to pay off his credit card debt. He never made any money from his documentaries. He often lost money on them."[5] Carpenter has vivid recollections of the Buick: "I remember when Jack bought that Buick. He drove it to meet me for a shoot, and I asked him about the big magnetic Razorback ornaments that were stuck randomly around the exterior. He showed me how he was using them to hide big areas where the paint was missing."

These observations may inadvertently make more comprehensible the occasional editorial lapses and slow moments in the films: they might in most instances be best understood as rooted in money. Working on *Arkansas' Hemingway*, for example, Hill may have realized as he edited his footage back in Little Rock that he was coming up short. In such a moment, he would have faced a difficult choice. The historian with a camera would wish to return to Piggott or at least do an additional background interview with another expert. An improved final cut would have surely resulted. But the producer at the helm of a one-man company with its head barely above water might be acutely conscious of added production costs involved and settle for a second look at footage from the cutting-room floor. Hill's remarkable output, it becomes clear, was driven in part by economic imperatives. He had to keep one eye on the money.

The Arkansas Series

Living alone in Little Rock apartments, Hill, in his last decade or so, pursued a nearly monastic life, throwing himself into long-deferred work opportunities that now beckoned. He had by this time secured additional regular supporters. In May of 1996, Arkansas Educational Television Network (AETN) contracted to pay him $2,000 for broadcast rights to fifteen separate titles, ten already completed and five then in production. Three of the finished works were films in a *What's Working* series that by 2000 totaled eight titles. Four others explored historical topics, and two of this group, *War in the Delta* and *War in the South*, were devoted to the Civil War.

But among the five titles listed in the AETN agreement as unfinished in May and due by December was one initially called *Black Gold in Arkansas* but eventually retitled as *Arkansas' Black Gold*. It was an unusually compelling early effort in the topic area that would emerge over time as Hill's true wheelhouse. Like *Red Bugs and Scholarships*, it credits an impressive list of local and state-level sponsors, but here the topic broadens to cover a tumultuous era in a whole section of southwestern and south-central Arkansas. The treatment edges away from Hill's standard three-segment structure toward a more sustained narrative arc he would perfect in subsequent films. The "black gold" at the film's center is oil, and when the Busey-Mitchell-Armstrong No. 1 well came in near the Union County town of El Dorado in 1920, it set off a spectacular "oil boom" throughout the area. Later Union County strikes at El Dorado and Smackover in 1921 and 1922 only added to the stampede. People slept in tents, in chicken coops, on porches, and in barns; barbers rented out their chairs at night.

Arkansas' Black Gold presents this turbulent story effectively, mixing archival photographs with the memories of senior citizens who were children during the boom times (though the film closes with footage of 1990s drilling rigs to demonstrate that oil is still being drilled and refined in South Arkansas). Historian Dee Brown, of *Bury My Heart at Wounded Knee* fame, was an unusually good interview—his mother was the postmistress at Stephens, where oil was also discovered in 1920, and her son's boyhood memories of exponentially upping his weekly tip income from carrying special-delivery letters to their addressees were still vivid seventy-five years later. His mother was too busy to notice, Brown recalled, that he was buying up the whole town's supply of licorice sticks.

Three years later, in 1999, Hill took a very similar approach to a different kind of gold, moving north and east to the Grand Prairie region of the state to produce *Arkansas' Grain*, a celebration of the state's nation-leading role in rice production. Once more the broad regional scope is fleshed out by closeup accounts of individuals, though *Arkansas' Grain* has little of the "bygone days" flavor so prominent in *Arkansas' Black Gold*. Arkansas is booming *now* (and was booming in 1999) as a rice-producing state. Yet another effort in this historically focused group was 2001's *Steamboat's a Comin'*, chronicling the glory days of big boats on Arkansas rivers and the important role of river transport in the development of the upper White River country of north-central Arkansas.

Arkansas' Grain features a spectacular instance of the director's relative indifference to the video tracks, especially for a person working in a visual medium. It's true that in several films viewers are occasionally brought up short by the apparent irrelevance of this or that odd shot. A whole segment of the 2003 *Arkansas' Hemingway* suddenly veers away from the account of the celebrated author to an extended tour of a quilt show. An interview with a security guard in 2009's *Faces like Ours* includes a bizarre shot tracking upward from the speaker's face to his cap with the word "POLICE" stitched on its front. These instances pale, however, in comparison to a sequence in *Arkansas' Grain*. The imposing husband-and-wife tombstone of Mr. and Mrs. W. H. Fuller in the Carlisle cemetery describes the couple as "Father and Mother of the Rice Industry in Arkansas." The parental metaphor applied to a major regional industry is comic from the start, but Hill cites the inscription only in the audio track. The video, meanwhile, includes a shot of the cemetery with the Fullers' stone prominent in the middle distance—it's the boss monument of the whole place, visible from the road if you know what you're looking for. But after all the buildup, Hill skips the money shot. (So glaring was this omission that research for this project included a trip to Carlisle, where we photographed the inscription for ourselves.)

These examples make a general point too emphatically. Such lapses are infrequent. Hill characteristically pays careful attention to harmonizing audio and video tracks, but the narrative element is invariably his primary focus. The visuals are significant but secondary—the pictures illustrate the words. For his part, cameraman Carpenter suspects that so striking an omission "could be a mistake or an oversight." "Editing was not Jack's strong suit," Carpenter continues, "but he edited all of his films quickly. He would rent a simple 'cuts-only' video editor by the hour, so time was always a factor. As the photogra-

Mother and father of the rice industry of Arkansas.
Photograph by Don House.

pher, I remember often being frustrated by some of
the editing choices made in the finished films."

This basic observation could be made more pos-
itively by focusing on Hill's striking skills as an oral
history interviewer. In film after film, his journalistic experience as a get-the-story reporter makes his
nose for the ideal interviewee extraordinarily acute.
Two examples will serve to make the point. In *Doing
What Was Right*, from 2004, sensing in Joe Ferguson
a perfect student-level match to Dale Bumpers's
school-board-lawyer perspective on the Charleston
school desegregation story, Hill added a shoot on
his jobsite in Mobile, Alabama. From both men Hill
elicited moving testimonies (they choke up while

speaking to him), effectively conveying old pains endured and current pride in their accomplishments.

Two years earlier, celebrating the various nineteenth-century immigrant communities who settled the Arkansas River Valley in *The Arkansas Runs through It*, he not only did a more-than-ten-minute sustained interview with ninety-three-year-old Alpha English but also edited it into a separate short entitled *Alpha English Remembers the All-Black Town of Menifee*. Here too, on what must have been brief acquaintance, Hill recognized Mrs. English as a remarkably knowledgeable and articulate source. He almost certainly did not know the details—that she graduated from both high school and college (where she was president of the Latin Club and news editor of the school paper) at Atlanta's famed Spelman College before returning to Menifee to teach school for more than thirty years. Twenty-five years before their interview she had co-authored a history of the town, *Menifee: Past and Present*. She lived to be one hundred, dying in 2008, and today she survives most vividly and durably in Hill's film and the more extended interview preserved in the University of Arkansas Library's Special Collections Division.

Here, yet again, was a perfectly positioned down-on-the ground narrator for the story he wished to tell, and he was quick to appreciate her importance. If the novelty of Hillary Rodham's breezy assurance and lack of makeup rattled him, Hill was back on familiar ground with Alpha English and Joe Ferguson. He'd gone to Mobile for Joe Ferguson's Charleston story, and he took time to record and edit an extended interview with Alpha English. Conscious of cost constraints, Hill may at times have edited quickly and padded out films with less than compelling visual

Alpha English's grave marker, Menifee Cemetery, Menifee, Arkansas. *Photograph by Sabine Schmidt.*

sequences (though his use of archival photographs is almost invariably effective). But when the story itself needed following to its source, he spared neither time nor money.

Arkansas History in the Schools

There's no way now to assess the degree of possible connection, but it also seems clear that Hill's increased focus on the state's social and economic history dovetailed nicely with larger movements in the world of public education. In 1997 the Arkansas legislature enacted a law requiring public schools to include the state's history in elementary and junior-high instruction, specifying that a full-semester course be developed for seventh- or eighth-grade classes. Hill was quick to sense a role for his films in filling gaps in the curricular resources available to teachers with novel responsibilities. In April of 1999, Walmart came through again, this time awarding more than $70,000 to place a set of eleven of Hill's Arkansas history titles in every public library and public-school media center in the state. (Hill got more than he'd asked for in this proposal—he'd envisioned the school media centers; the Walton folks added the libraries.)

By 2003, he was ready with a follow-up proposal, this one for a twelve-title roster explicitly labeled the "Arkansas Series," calling for a total of more than nineteen thousand tapes of the films to be distributed free of charge to the same recipients. The sheer scale of this project suggests Hill's increased confidence in the significance of his work—as does the hortatory tone that occasionally surfaces in the rhetoric of his proposals. "The history of Arkansas is as colorful and dramatic as any state," he writes in the 2003 proposal. "We just didn't know it."[6]

This note also surfaces in the stand-up introductions to individual films. *The Arkansas Runs through It*, a 2002 title, opens well north of the river at the annual Grape Festival in Tontitown before concentrating its attention on the African American community of Menifee in Conway County; the Polish, Czech, and German settlements around Dardanelle (Yell County) and Marche (Pulaski County); and the more recent Hispanic and Vietnamese arrivals in Clarksville (Johnson County) and Fort Smith (Sebastian County). Noting that despite growing up in nearby Rogers, he's never before attended the festival in Tontitown, Hill generalizes his own experience:

"It's sort of a story of Arkansas, isn't it? We're not that familiar with the history in our own backyard."

This neglected heritage, Arkansas's "backyard" history, forms the core of Hill's work in the final decade of his life. The "Arkansas Series" label stuck once he'd hit on it to describe his current projects. It's of course true that virtually every film he produced from the start was devoted to some aspect of Arkansas life. Even the most obvious exceptions, *To Russia with Love* and the several related films dealing with a struggling Christian congregation in Yekaterinburg, Russia, and a United Methodist seminary in Moscow, were at bottom accounts of outreach efforts by Hill's own Methodist congregation in Little Rock. They were also Arkansas stories, despite the international settings.

But when Hill used the name "Arkansas Series," he also meant to single out the wider-angled, history-based titles he'd developed beginning with *Arkansas' Black Gold* in 1996 and the even earlier *Work Will Win* in 1994. These were where he planted his flag as a documentary filmmaker, and his pride in what he'd accomplished is evident in the unusually celebratory prose he wrote to promote them. A proposal draft preserved in Hill's papers—it's undated but appears to be centered on *The Arkansas Runs through It*—displays this tone with unusual élan. The proposed new film is first tied to other titles in an "Arkansas Series" regarded as already established. Various sponsorship levels, with prices, are then laid out, with everything leading up to Hill's close, set off under a "The Final Word" heading: "No other state, not one, will have a comparable video resource for promoting education."[7] It's yet another *We're*

Number One!, this one with Hill's own work leading the nation.

The contract with AETN in 1996 might be seen as another milepost in Hill's reinvention of himself. By the time of its execution, he had managed, thanks to sustained support from Walmart and other sponsors, to produce nearly thirty films and arrange for their broadcast on a variety of commercial outlets. But with the AETN contract, he secured a long-term association with the statewide public television outlet, explicitly educational in its own mission, gaining regular and repeated broadcasts of his films. The basic shape of the contract is no less revealing—half the money to be paid is for unlimited showings of ten films already completed, but the second installment is for five projects in the pipeline, underway but not yet finished. AETN isn't really risking its funds on Hill's timely delivery—payment is to be made only upon the receipt of all five. What is at least implicitly assumed, however, is their quality. By 1996, Hill is clearly perceived as both dependable and competent. The contract, for all its legal hedges, radiates confidence—Hill will get his work done, it says, and we'll be proud to have our name affixed to its public airing. Six months after its signing, the November issue of the *AETN Program Guide* mailed to patrons featured a "Jack Hill Productions on AETN" piece listing prime-time slots for three films as part of "an effort to bring more Arkansas programming to our viewers." The filmmaker's motives were made explicit: "In allowing AETN to air his productions, Hill said he wants Arkansans to be more familiar with their state and take pride in its colorful history and unique environment."[8]

Jump forward almost another decade, and Hill's reputation is such that each new release is regularly noted in the press. In 2005, when Hill completed *Wings of Honor*, his portrait of the World War II–era heyday of the Walnut Ridge Army Flying School, *Arkansas Democrat-Gazette* writer Michael Storey plugged it in his The TV Column as the "latest fascinating and educational special from producer/reporter Jack Hill's TeleVision for Arkansas series." Storey also provided details of the film's four-barreled debut: "*Wings of Honor* airs today at 12:30 p.m. on KHBS-TV in Fort Smith and KHOG-TV in Fayetteville; and at 1:30 p.m. on KATV in Little Rock. AETN viewers can see the program at 9:30 p.m. Thursday, with encores at 6:30 p.m. Friday and 9:30 p.m. June 13."[9] This is PR gold—good coverage on the print publicity front promoting wider exposure over the airwaves.

Hill kept Storey busy the following year, when he released three new films, beginning with *New Schools for Arkansas* in January. Similar to *Work Will Win* from the previous decade but much wider in its scope, it focused not on the single Fargo Agricultural School in Monroe County but on the nearly four hundred Rosenwald Schools constructed in forty-six Arkansas counties in support of African American education. Funding help came from Sears president and philanthropist Julius Rosenwald. The new schools are old now—most are gone and only Dunbar Magnet Middle School in Little Rock still hosts classes, but Hill sought out and filmed several surviving structures, often with interviews and guided tours led by former students. These elders testifying to the encouragement offered at critical junctures are the film's highlights—Storey's review is a rave, and he's already seen enough of Hill's films to single out their most appealing features for positive comment: "As with most of his productions, Hill presents a number of folks chatting about the subject and how it personally touched their lives."[10] As in the *Wings of Honor* story, the AETN broadcast date and time are provided.

Storey's coverage of *Arsenal for Democracy*, Hill's story of the World War II–era Arkansas Ordnance Plant in Little Rock, released four months later, in May, was no less positive. A huge plant in its days of peak operation in 1942–43, it employed more than fourteen thousand workers, mostly women. Storey, quoting Hill, describes the plant's significance: "'What happened here also helped win a war,' he notes. 'Eighty-eight percent of the detonators and relays in all American bombs in World War II were made at the facility.'" Storey describes the film itself as "fascinating," provides broadcast dates and times, and notes that Hill "chats with several who remember their days fondly."[11] Storey didn't have the space for details, but here the "chats with several" line understates dramatically Hill's response to one chat in particular. One of the plant's employees had used her lunch breaks, every day, to write a letter to a soldier, sailor, or airman. She had saved their grateful replies, and by the time Hill interviewed her more than half a century later, she had hundreds, carefully ordered in her home. Hill devotes what must have been unanticipated time (and an added shoot location) to capturing the full impact of her story. Instances of oral history conducted with such nuanced skill are regular features of his films.

Hill's next effort was *Currents of History*, aired in

October as the third 2006 release. This one moves farther back in time to examine the impact of Randolph County rivers as nineteenth-century settlement arteries—one was the Current River, punned on in the title. "Hill's half-hour special reports are always enlightening and usually surprising," Storey writes, "as they highlight little-known nuggets of Arkansas history." He then quotes Hill restating his standard call for wider attention to such nuggets: "'We have more history in Arkansas than most of us realize,' he says. 'It may not go back as far as here in Randolph County, but it's here if we take the time to find it.'" *Currents of History* is "a visual treat," Storey concludes, adding that "the best moments are when those connected to the history of the places have their say."[12] Here, as with the rock-throwing codgers of *Arkansas' Hemingway* or the pen-pal ordnance plant worker of *Arsenal for Democracy* with her hundreds of home-archived letters, is Hill at his best, ear alert for the story little known because too often overlooked. Storey again provides broadcast dates and times.

Storey also produced rave notices for the 2009 *Faces like Ours*, Hill's exploration of the World War II POW camps that housed some twenty-three thousand captured German and Italian soldiers, and for *The Long Walk*, his 2010 Trail of Tears account of the forced removal of Choctaws from their Alabama and Mississippi homelands to the "Indian Territory" in present-day Oklahoma. The former gets the biggest spread of Storey's pieces—there's even a still of German prisoners arriving under guard at Camp Robinson—but he reserved special praise for *The Long Walk*, calling it "one of Hill's most informative and visually compelling specials in the 16 years I've been watching them."[13]

No Escape Velocity

The Long Walk was the final film Hill produced by himself. When it appeared at the end of 2010, Hill had a year and a half to live, and he would devote the best of those days to working on *War in the '60s,* a film recognized from the start as his last. His end came suddenly, and it came in the wake of another great loss. Jack's father, Radus Hill, had died in 1989 at seventy-eight, just as his son was getting started with TeleVision for Arkansas. Grace Fields Hill, however, lived another twenty years, witnessing her son's steady run of successful films (and all the while continuing to enjoy Christmas visits with Jack and Anne). She was ninety-six when she died at the end of January in 2012. Only "a few days later," according to the obituary tribute composed by former KAIT co-anchor Becky Allison, Hill was himself diagnosed with kidney cancer. His struggles with his own health may explain the four-month delay in arranging for his mother's funeral in May, but her obituary notice, composed by Hill, quietly sustained the story he and Anne had nourished through a decade of Christmas visits. "Grace is survived," he wrote, "by her son Jack Hill and wife, Anne, of Little Rock."[14]

Hill returned to Rogers for his own treatments, where his mother's great friend and fellow teacher Bonnie Grimes helped when he needed care, and returned to his Little Rock apartment when he felt better to devote himself to editing *War in the '60s.* He died there suddenly, on July 12, not directly from cancer but from internal bleeding following a fall. Anne Hill, taking up in her turn the obit writer's pen, returned the favor: "When I wrote his [obituary] I listed me, 'his wife of thirty-seven years.'"[15]

Hill's friends, gathered in Little Rock for a service in his memory, praised his life of service and laughed together at the stubborn eccentricities of character that he'd wrestled into assets in that life. Longtime cameraman Dale Carpenter's eulogy included at its close an anecdote capturing this achievement perfectly:

> We were shooting a documentary about the Battle of Pea Ridge, and we're out on Old Wire Road early one morning where the soldiers marched into battle. Jack says he needs a 30-second walking shot to cover a quote from a soldier describing the march. It was a section that looked like it could be 1862—just trees and dirt road. So I put the camera on my shoulder looked around at the light and said, "Jack, I'm going to do the shot walking this way because the light's a lot better."
>
> Jack's response was, "But they were going that way."
>
> "Yeah, I know, but it's going to look so much better this way, and no one will be able to tell which direction I'm going on video."
>
> Jack smiled and looked at me and said, "But Dale, they were marching that way."
>
> Exasperated, I said, "Okay, I'm going to shoot it both ways, and you pick the one you like best in editing."
>
> For those of you who knew Jack, I don't have to tell you which shot he used . . . because they *were* marching that way. For Jack it was always truth before beauty, although he appreciated good video, too.[16]

Listening from her front-row pew, Anne might have recognized a parallel instance, this one sustained through a decade's annual reiterations, of Jack's literalist sense of "truth before beauty": "He had a Christmas list consisting of about 100 people from different periods of his life. During all those years of our separation, he insisted on tracking me down and having me sign my name to the cards. I asked him many times to forge my name but he would never do that. No matter what was going on, I had to sign my 'Anne' to the cards while he stood there waiting."[17]

The man on Old Wire Road, these lovely anecdotes reveal, was among other things an adult version of the toddler on the couch with the volumes of Civil War history (and something, too, of the director of *Arkansas' Grain* in the Carlisle cemetery). His stiff demeanor drove spouse, colleagues, and camera operators crazy, and he was the last man you'd want to run into at a party. But he was a stellar scout in Dr. Asperger's earnest troop (think full sash of merit badges, proudly worn). Trustworthy, loyal, helpful, friendly—he bought the whole dodecalogue, hook and line. His school-principal mother and war-hero father raised their only child to a God-and-country credo and a social-gospel Methodist faith, and though he sometimes paid a stiff price for such unrelieved high-mindedness, that son rarely wavered and never recanted. Union blue and Razorback red were always his colors. Two years after his death, in May of 2014, AETN aired the completed *War in the '60s* as TeleVision for Arkansas's longest film. With final editing by Carpenter, it recycled the very footage at the center of his memorial service anecdote (from the 1992 *War Comes to Arkansas*). The soldiers were still marching that way.

Regarded from a stand-back-and-take-in-the-whole-bio vantage point, Hill's life and career exhibit a clearly defined out-and-back arc. He planned from at least his high school years for a career in broadcast journalism and from at least his army stint in Germany and graduate work in Missouri for a focus on national and international stories. Arkansas stories, and the Arkansas history behind those stories, were absent from his screen. But then, following a string of early disappointments in Colorado, Mississippi, and Texas, he landed back in Arkansas for a magical decade in Jonesboro followed by twice that time as a pioneering Arkansas documentary filmmaker. If there's a pivotal film, a eureka moment where the still-novice producer-director experiences a sense of finding wholly engrossing work to fully engage his talents and energies, the best guess might locate it in 1994, with *Work Will Win*'s sustained celebration of the Fargo Agricultural School's underdog achievements on behalf of educational opportunities for spectacularly underserved African American students in the Arkansas Delta. "I think Dr. Brown had us in mind," recalled Fargo student Sylvester Green of Dr. Brown's tireless and often humiliating fundraising efforts on behalf of his fledgling school, and it seems clear that Hill was inspired in his subsequent work by the Browns' mostly unremarked achievement. He had Joe Six-Pack in his mind. Not only would Arkansas stories with a conspicuous historical dimension dominate his subsequent efforts, but their telling would inspire his most vividly realized, coherently focused films.

It's a rare Hill piece that doesn't include at least one or two anecdotal high points—his skills as an interviewer time and again elicit deeply personal (if sometimes sharply painful) accounts. An absolutely apex moment occurs in one of his otherwise pedestrian *Education in the Workplace* pieces, when a Georgia-Pacific employee in Crossett searches for adequate words to express his gratitude to the reading specialist whose diagnosis of his dyslexia allowed him to complete a company-sponsored GED program. After only "my Lord and my wife," he tells the camera, the just-awarded certificate is his greatest treasure. It's magnificent, a drop-the-mic moment. But films like *A Place Called Home*, *Arsenal for Democracy*, *Doing What Was Right*, *Dollar a Day and All You Can Eat*, *New Schools for Arkansas*, *Water Steals the Land: Arkansas' Great Flood*, and *Wings of Honor* join with *Work Will Win* in situating similar highlights in effectively contextualized larger narratives. They make up the very best of Hill's work.

"A lot of people leave Arkansas," Charles Portis writes in *The Dog of the South*, "and most of them come back sooner or later. They can't quite achieve escape velocity."[18] Hill went all the way to Moscow, scurried busily over nearly the whole of Europe, and devoted a year to studying network television's coverage of the war in Vietnam in preparation for a planned career as a globe-trotting television journalist. But as it turned out, no big-world stories had for him the drawing power of the Fargo Agricultural School, the oil boom in El Dorado and Smackover, the Rosenwald Schools scattered across Arkansas, the Rosie the Riveter tales of women breaking into the workforce at the Arkansas Ordnance Plant in Jacksonville, the boys-to-men tales of the Civilian Conservation Corps's building the Arkansas State Parks system from the ground up, or the quiet heroism of the African American community and the school board of Charleston in 1954.

Charleston High School National Commemorative Site.
Photograph by Don House.

National and international plans were long since shoved aside by such local and regional sagas by the time he came up with his Arkansas Series. Work did win, for Hill as much as for the Browns and their students, and nothing attracted him more than narratives highlighting the fabulous, saga-like character of undercelebrated lives constructed outside the limelight of the larger world's attention. It's clear the folks running the Arkansas Historical Association chose wisely in bestowing their just-in-time 2012 award, and now, a decade later, it's high time for Jack Hill's Arkansas films to light up the state's screens again.

PART II

THE FILMS

THE ARKANSAS SERIES

We have ordered chronologically the sixteen films plus two clips selected from (and in at least one instance added to) the Arkansas Series as Hill conceived it. Sixteen films is a large selection, approximately 25 percent of Hill's total output as an independent film-maker. It is not, however, in any respect a random selection, and it reflects several editorial decisions on our part made in recognition of plausible alternatives. Our choices might at times appear idiosyncratic.

Hill made *My Brother's Keeper* in 1994 in response to the AIDS epidemic in Arkansas—a strikingly courageous film given the hysterias of the day. He also completed a whole series of films on a wide range of other public health issues particularly troublesome in Arkansas (strokes, obesity, childhood hunger, low-birth-weight babies). On number of titles alone, we could have plausibly portrayed him as centrally concerned with such matters. Hill was also a devout man, a lifelong Methodist especially active in his home church's outreach missions to the Russia he'd been so eager to visit as a serviceman—the making of *To Russia with Love* in 1997 and *Opportunity for Mission in Russia* in 2001 took him back for two additional visits. Closer to home, his *Keeping the Faith* in 1996 involved widespread travels to film Jewish congregations in Jonesboro, Catholics in McGehee, and Protestants in Washington. Faith-related topics were clearly another core area of interest. He was also attracted to sports, though athletic topics are invariably subordinated to educational issues in Hill's sports-centered titles. Given this range, our selection of history-based narratives as the foundation of Hill's accomplishment may be defensible and perhaps even obvious but not wholly inevitable.

The overall trajectory of his career as a documentary filmmaker from 1989 through 2012 also exhibits a marked increase in quality over time. This is especially clear in the growing confidence of his approach to longer narrative arcs combining contemporary settings and interviews with various archival resources. But within the Arkansas Series itself, such development is less clear. *Arkansas' Grain* comes early in the sequence, yet it is one of Hill's most tightly constructed efforts; *Work Will Win* was completed before Hill conceived the Arkansas Series, but viewed in conjunction with later works, it holds its place well. It seems to us one of his finest efforts. *The Long Walk* and *Arkansas' Hemingway*, both later films, might seem slow-paced or even meandering by comparison.

Once he found his favored topics, Hill characteristically worked at a pace slowed only slightly from the breakneck speed of his work on the early titles devoted to public health and adult education topics in the 1990s. For each title selected, we provide here a brief contextual reprise (locations, air dates, sponsors, interviewees) with appended anecdotes, appraisals and reviews, comparative observations.

To access the streaming-video component of

Reporting for Arkansas, please visit https://arkstudies .uark.edu/publications/jack-hill/videos/. As of press time, permission to include *The Attack* has not yet been granted by Gray Television, owners of KAIT. If and when this happens, the video clip will be uploaded.

Work Will Win

YEAR OF RELEASE: 1994.

SOURCE: Betacam SP cassette, MC 1355, series 2, box 2T, tape 17, Jack Hill Papers, University of Arkansas Library Special Collections Division (hereafter cited as UA Special Collections).

CAMERA: Dale Carpenter.

TITLE: Michael Murphy. Announcer: Rusty Black. Production Coordinator: Mike Narisi. Postproduction: Anthony May.

PRODUCTION: Hailstone Creek Productions, Light Productions.

SPONSORS: Arkansas Department of Parks and Tourism, Arkansas Humanities Council, Electric Cooperatives of Arkansas, Fargo Agricultural School Reunion, Georgia-Pacific, Heifer Project International, National Endowment for the Humanities, Phillips Petroleum Company, Points of Light Foundation, Southwestern Bell Telephone, University of Arkansas at Pine Bluff, Walmart, Winthrop Rockefeller Foundation.

INTERVIEWS: Jack Adams, Elmer Burnett, Tolbert Chism, Junior Coleman, Geraldine Davidson, Othello Faison, Minnie Farr, Sylvester Green, Calvin King, Harlan London, Ulysses Marshall, Sarah Jean O'Neal, Magnolia Tounsel.

Work Will Win was not Hill's first film to focus on a historical topic—this would be *War Comes to Arkansas*, from 1992. But in the decidedly less well-known story of the Fargo Agricultural School's pioneering efforts in offering improved educational opportunities to African American children, Hill found a topic perfectly suited to his interests, his convictions, and his talents. His concern with education had been evident as early as his letter home from his Cold War visit to the Russian school, and his involvement with civil rights issues went back at least to his interviews with students at recently integrated high schools in Jackson in the 1970s. His enthusiasm for the story of the heroic, pioneering educational efforts of Floyd and Lillie Epps Brown in Fargo is palpable, and viewers today might sense *Work Will Win* as the film where Hill comes fully into his mission as a filmmaker for the first time. He bills its subject as one of African American Arkansas's "great stories of accomplishment against all odds."

These "odds" included a racist social regime then solidly entrenched—when President Brown went north on his fundraising trips, he carried with him letters of introduction from Arkansas governors conveying explicit assurance that "nothing in the training" offered at Fargo was designed "to instill false ideas of the proper relationship of the races." (Ponder this with the advantages of nearly a century's hindsight—the supersize helpings of shame and rage this dedicated teacher was made to swallow financing high school diplomas for his charges.)

Dale Carpenter's memories of the filming sessions remain vivid a quarter century later: "Jack found this story—it was completely new to me.

My family is from East Arkansas. My grandmother lived in Brinkley, but I had never heard of the Fargo Agricultural School. When we shot the reunion, I remember being amazed at how important the school had been to so many African Americans, who came from all over the state for their high school education."

And then returned from all over the nation for their reunions—*Work Will Win* includes closeup shots of auto license plates from Indiana, Michigan, and New Jersey, as well as footage of an FAS graduate at work as a department chair at Syracuse University ("Syracuse was cold!" Carpenter remembers). Hill's film is old enough now to possess, in addition to its merits as an effective documentary film, a striking archival value. The proud Fargo Agricultural School graduates he interviewed in 1993 were in their sixties and seventies then—they're mostly gone now, and Jack Hill's film record is thereby doubly precious.

What remains in Fargo and is still busily active in educational and social service efforts is the Arkansas Land and Community Development Corporation (ALCDC). Dr. Calvin King, its executive director and CEO, explicitly understands himself as carrying forward Dr. Brown's large legacy—the Floyd Brown–Fargo Agricultural School Museum is housed within ALCDC facilities. Dr. King knew Hill well, served as the primary source in his 1984 KAIT program, *Black Farmers in Arkansas: A Tradition Disappears*, and was featured prominently in *Work Will Win*. Our visit to Fargo in May 2021 was one of this project's highlight experiences.

Dr. Calvin King at the Floyd Brown–Fargo Agricultural
School Museum, Fargo, Arkansas, May 18, 2021.
Photograph by Don House.

Additional Resources

Chatman, Kae. "Fargo Agricultural School." In *Encyclopedia
of Arkansas*. Central Arkansas Library System, 2006–.
Article last modified June 8, 2016. https://encyclopedia
ofarkansas.net/entries/fargo-agricultural-school-2375/.

Fargo Agricultural School Collection. MG.02864. Microfilm
collection. Arkansas State Archives.

Floyd Brown–Fargo Agricultural School Museum. Floyd
Brown Drive, Fargo, AR 72021.

Arkansas' Black Gold

YEAR OF RELEASE: 1996.

SOURCE: Betacam SP cassette, broadcast tape, aired June 1996, on AETN, box 52, Jack Hill Papers, UA Special Collections.

CAMERA: Dale Carpenter.

TITLE: Michael Murphy. Announcer: Rusty Black. Production Coordinator: Joanne Elliott. Postproduction: Light Productions.

SPONSORS: Alice-Sidney Oil Company, Arkansas Department of Parks and Tourism, Arkansas Oil and Brine Museum, Best Western Kings Inn Conference Center, ENSCO, Langley Oil Company, Lion Oil Company El Dorado Refinery, Reliance Well Service of Magnolia, Smackover State Bank, State Farm Insurance, Stephens Chamber of Commerce, Stephens Security Bank, United Methodist Church, Walmart.

INTERVIEWS: E. Boyd Alderson, Dee Brown, Hamp Bussey, Essie Butler, Gary Davis, Ruben Dees, Don Lambert, Catherine Linkous, Ralph Linkous, Hayden McBride, W. T. Newton.

Arkansas' Black Gold appears in retrospect as a second film where Hill really found his sweet spot as a history-focused Arkansas filmmaker. He had a lot going for him. His topic was the biggest economic boom story in the state's history (his lead-in compares it to the nineteenth-century gold rushes), his on-camera authorities (Dee Brown and Don Lambert) were unusually effective narrators, and in Ruben Dees he found the first of his truly top-notch oral history interviewees (in the same league with Gloria Counts of *Arsenal for Democracy*, Joe Ferguson of *Doing What Was Right*, and Alpha English of *The Arkansas Runs through It*).

The result is an effectively ordered chronicle of the 1920s oil bonanza in South Arkansas, a time of upheaval at once wonderful and terrible, its vivid interviews accompanied by informative archival photographs and news clips. And Hill will get even better—several *Black Gold* interviews come across as lifeless booster boilerplate. Empty suits will mostly disappear from later titles, their sanitized office spaces replaced by homes and yards where salt-of-the-earth folks relate first-person experience with plain eloquence.

Additional Resources

Bridges, Kenneth. "Oil Industry." In *Encyclopedia of Arkansas*. Central Arkansas Library System, 2006–. Article last modified December 21, 2017. https://encyclopediaofarkansas.net/entries/oil-industry-383/.

Brown, Dee. *When the Century Was Young*. Little Rock: August House, 1993. See esp. chap. 2, "Oil Booms and Flimflammers."

Martel, Glen. "Oil and Gas in Southwest Arkansas." *Arkansas Historical Quarterly* 4, no. 3 (Autumn 1945): 196–214.

The Newest Arkansans

YEAR OF RELEASE: 1999.

SOURCE: Betacam SP cassette, broadcast tape, aired April 29, 1999, on AETN, box 52, Jack Hill Papers, UA Special Collections.

CAMERA: Dale Carpenter.

TITLE: Michael Murphy. Announcer: Rusty Black. Production Coordinator: Lee Burrell. Postproduction: Light Productions.

SPONSORS: Arkansas Community Foundation, Electric Cooperatives of Arkansas, Northwest Arkansas Regional Airport, Walmart.

INTERVIEWS: Bobby Bell, Bill Brown, José Dominguez, Dan Ferritor, Greg Fike, Roland Goicoechea, Jeff Harper, Gail Isabel, Marsha Jones, Ramiro Lizcano, Al Lopez, Maria Morales, Jon Nathan, David Nations, Ed Nicholson, Lorenzo Reyes, Jim Rollins, John Sampier, Doug Sarver, Connie Velasquez, Perry Webb.

The Newest Arkansans might be best approached as a Hill-comes-home film, as its geographical focus is almost wholly limited to Northwest Arkansas, with significant segments filmed in his hometown of Rogers. One classroom scene takes place in the Grace F. Hill Elementary School, named in honor of his mother, and another brief sequence featuring an old Rogers High yearbook might well have used Hill's personal copy. The "newest Arkansans" of the title are Spanish-speaking immigrants who came in such numbers in the 1990s that Arkansas then led the nation in the growth rate of its Hispanic population.

The tone of Hill's portrayal is resolutely upbeat (though alarmist news stories of rising crime rates are mentioned, the better to be refuted), with multiple instances of newly welcoming arrangements in area schools, workplaces, public recreation programs, and churches. University of Arkansas sociologist Dan Ferritor opens and closes the film as its academic expert, but Hill's larger than usual interview list (at least twenty-one interviewees, though not all are named with Hill's standard subtitles) gives primary voice to the recent arrivals themselves and the pastors, teachers, and workplace supervisors who welcome them. A Springdale teacher named Lorenzo Reyes may be the film's real star—we see him as a role model, leading his classes, but he started as a tomato and watermelon picker who worked in the fields of Alma and Van Buren from dawn until lunchtime and went to college in the afternoon.

Additional Resources

Capps, Randy, Kristen McCabe, Michael Fix, and Ying Huang. *Changing Workforce and Family Demographics*. Vol. 1 of *A Profile of Immigrants in Arkansas*. Little Rock: Winthrop Rockefeller Foundation; Washington, DC: Migration Policy Institute, 2013.

Leidermann, Michel. "Latinos." In *Encyclopedia of Arkansas*. Central Arkansas Library System, 2006–. Article last modified July 7, 2021. https://encyclopediaofarkansas. net/entries/latinos-2733/.

Arkansas' Grain

YEAR OF RELEASE: 1999.

SOURCE: Betacam SP cassette, broadcast tape, aired December 5, 1999, on KATV, box 42, Jack Hill Papers, UA Special Collections.

CAMERAS: Dale Carpenter, Leonard Chamblee.

TITLE: Michael Murphy. Announcer: Rusty Black. Postproduction: Light Productions.

SPONSORS: Arkansas Delta Byways, Arkansas Farm Bureau Federation, Arkansas Rice Council, Arkansas Rice Research and Promotion Board, Arkansas State University College of Agriculture, Electric Cooperatives of Arkansas, Farmers and Merchants Bank of Stuttgart, Producers Rice Mill, Riceland Foods, Stuttgart Agricultural Museum, Walmart.

INTERVIEWS: Bennie Burkett, Wayne Clow, David Jessup, Dolores Jessup, Gene Jessup, Stewart Jessup, Pat Peacock, John Robinson, Neil Rutger, L. F. Seidenstricker, Leonard Sitzer, Mrs. Carl Yohe.

Hill's portrayal of the Arkansas rice industry emerges as a clear reprise of the approach taken in 1996's *Arkansas' Black Gold*, where Hill for the first time focused on the central economic industry associated with a particular region. Where the emphasis there was historical, on a South Arkansas boom-time era seventy years old at the time of filming, *Arkansas' Grain* focuses on Grand Prairie action in the 1999 present. From a slightly different perspective, however, *Arkansas' Grain*, with its extended focus on a single large-scale family operation near Lodge Corner in Arkansas County, exhibits close ties to one of Hill's initial efforts in independent filmmaking, the 1990 *Two Families*. Hill was an old hand at combining the two—even as a newsman in Jackson, he'd learned to present big-issue topics from a down-on-the-ground vantage point (as when he'd interviewed local black and white high schoolers in Jackson on the hot-button topic of integrated classrooms).

He was also getting better at minimizing empty-suit booster interviews. Industry spokespersons appear in *Arkansas' Grain*, though here they're actual rice scientists, proud of the new higher-yield varieties helpful to the region's farmers. But already Hill is finding his richest lode of memorable interviews elsewhere, in this instance with Mrs. Carl Yohe's recollections of harvests, during which midday meals for twenty-man crews were prepared on wood-burning stoves, and L. F. Seidenstricker's if-you-grow-it-and-sell-it-you-should-eat-it credo. On their farm, even now, he says, they eat rice every day.

Additional Resources

Fuller, W. H. "Early Rice Farming on Grand Prairie." *Arkansas Historical Quarterly* 14, no. 1 (Spring 1955): 72–74.

Gates, John. "Groundwater Irrigation and the Development of the Grand Prairie Rice Industry." *Arkansas Historical Quarterly* 64 (Winter 2005): 394–413.

Teske, Steven. "Rice Industry." In *Encyclopedia of Arkansas*. Central Arkansas Library System, 2006–. Article last modified August 8, 2018. https://encyclopediaofarkansas. net/entries/rice-industry-380/.

Steamboat's a Comin'

YEAR OF RELEASE: 2001.

SOURCE: Betacam SP cassette, broadcast tape, aired April 2, 2001, on KAIT, box 7, Jack Hill Papers, UA Special Collections.

CAMERAS: Dale Carpenter, Leonard Chamblee.

TITLE: Michael Murphy. Announcer: Rusty Black. Postproduction: Light Productions.

SPONSORS: Arkansas Department of Parks and Tourism, Butler Center for Arkansas Studies, Department of Arkansas Heritage, Electric Cooperatives of Arkansas, Walmart.

INTERVIEWS: Claude Ashmore, Mark Christ, Edwin Luther, Johnny Murphy, Sammie Rose, Pat Wood.

The strengths of *Steamboat's a Comin'* are centered on its fluent transitions across widely separated sections of Arkansas and on Hill's increasing confidence in integrating archival stills into his live film sequences. The focus on steamboats echoes the oil wells of *Arkansas' Black Gold*—where the earlier film used their shared oil booms to link Stephens with El Dorado and Smackover, *Steamboat's a Comin'* deploys the common importance of steamboat traffic to link Batesville on the White River with Washington on the Red and Camden on the Ouachita. Only the Civil War films and perhaps *Water Steals the Land: Arkansas' Great Flood* so effectively utilize century-old images to vividly communicate the historical importance of their subjects.

Like the later *Arkansas' Hemingway, Steamboat's a Comin'* does run short of top-level footage, most evidently in a segment near the end devoted to a less-than-riveting tour of a refurbished White River workboat by members of the Arkansas Parks Commission. Throughout his career as an independent film producer, Hill worked under tight budget constraints. His careful planning and ingenuity in fitting clips from one film seamlessly into others account for the rarity of such threadbare moments.

Additional Resources

Dillard, Tom. "Introducing Steamboats to Arkansas." *Arkansas Democrat-Gazette*, April 12, 2020. https://www.arkansasonline.com/news/2020/apr/12/introducing-steamboats-to-arkansas-2020/.

Stewart-Abernathy, Leslie C. "Steamboats." In *Encyclopedia of Arkansas*. Central Arkansas Library System, 2006–. Article last modified January 16, 2019. https://encyclopediaofarkansas.net/entries/steamboats-4466/.

Water Steals the Land: Arkansas' Great Flood

YEAR OF RELEASE: 2002.

SOURCE: Betacam SP cassette, broadcast tape, aired April 28, 2002, on KATV, box 42, Jack Hill Papers, UA Special Collections.

CAMERAS: Dale Carpenter, Leonard Chamblee.

TITLE: Michael Murphy. Announcer: Rusty Black. Postproduction: Light Productions.

SPONSORS: Arkansas Humanities Council, Delta Cultural Center, Department of Arkansas Heritage.

INTERVIEWS: Ben Allen, Edyth Allen, Bob Anderson, Claude Ashmore, Verda Breedlove, Ken Carter, Ralph Cloar, Virginia Cloar, Haggard Crews, Lucie Davis, Michael Dougan, Eldon Fairley, Geraldine Grundy, Will Hendrix, Clarence Johnson, Louis Kealer, Naomi Lawson, Irene LeLouis, Dorothy Moore, Henry Pennymon, Delmer Plummer, Charlotte Schexnayder, Mattie Smiley, Willie Williams.

The seventy-fifth anniversary of Arkansas's most devastating flood saw one of Hill's best-funded films. A major grant from the Arkansas Humanities Council made possible a greatly shortened sponsor list (and a rare Hill effort not initiated with Walmart backing). The result is one of his best films, anchored in twenty-five wide-ranging interviews and stunning archival film footage effectively contextualized.

The sequences of flooded-out refugees standing in food lines and living in tent cities have a

Depression-era aura, making it starkly clear that many Arkansas were living in impoverished circumstances in 1927, two years before the crash came to Wall Street. The film's emphasis rightly falls on the state's eastern half, in the hardest-hit delta counties, but as usual Hill does his best to cast a statewide net. Shots of a washed-out railroad bridge in Little Rock and flooding as far west as Fort Smith are included.

Along with *Arkansas' Black Gold*, *Wings of Honor*, and the Civil War films, this fast-paced chronicle may possess the widest public appeal in the filmography of the man who billed himself as Arkansas's reporter in search of Joe Six-Pack.

Additional Resources

Daniel, Pete. *Deep'n as It Come: The 1927 Mississippi River Flood*. Fayetteville, AR: University of Arkansas Press, 1996.

Hendricks, Nancy. "Flood of 1927." In *Encyclopedia of Arkansas*. Central Arkansas Library System, 2006–. Article last modified April 17, 2017. https://encyclo pediaofarkansas.net/entries/flood-of-1927-2202/.

Simpson, Ethel C. "Letters from the Flood." *Arkansas Historical Quarterly* 55, no. 3 (Autumn 1996): 251–85.

The Arkansas Runs through It

YEAR OF RELEASE: 2002.

SOURCE: Betacam SP cassette, broadcast tape, aired
June 2, 2002, on KHBS-TV, box 14, Jack Hill Papers,
UA Special Collections.

CAMERA: Uncredited.

TITLE: Uncredited. Announcer: Uncredited.
Postproduction: Uncredited.

SPONSORS: Arkansas Department of Parks and
Tourism, Arkansas River Valley Tri-Peaks Region,
Butler Center for Arkansas Studies, Department of
Arkansas Heritage, Walmart.

INTERVIEWS: Ben Anderson, Kenneth Barnes, Alpha
English, Bill Franklin, Alice Hines, Arthur Kitta, Maggie
Kitta, Be Le, Do Van Le, Al Wiederkehr, Jonathan
Wolfe.

If history emerges as the most obvious signature
topic for Hill's films, his attraction to rivers might
make them a candidate for the runner-up spot.
He devotes one film to the great flood of 1927 and
another to the glory days of steamboat traffic on
the White River, while *Currents of History* focuses
on the role of four streams, punning on the name
of one, in the early settlement history of Northeast
Arkansas. *The Arkansas Runs through It* is different,
the river here used as a kind of necklace string to pull
the story of a series of immigrant communities from
the nineteenth century to the present into coherence.
It opens with Hill's stand-up intro in Northwest

Arkansas, at the annual Tontitown Grape Festival. Tontitown is nowhere close to the Arkansas River, but the town and the festival fit his subject perfectly, plus he had excellent footage left over from *The Newest Arkansans*. Plagiarizing yourself is no crime at all and good work if you can get it. The film then moves south to celebrate German and Swiss immigrant communities in Conway, Dixie, and Altus; the African American town of Menifee; and Czech and Polish settlements in Dardanelle, Danville, and Marche.

All these, like Tontitown, were established by nineteenth-century arrivals, but the film closes with more recently established Vietnamese and Hispanic communities in Fort Smith and Clarksville. *The Arkansas Runs through It* is one of Hill's fastest-paced films, but it never seems rushed. In Menifee's Alpha English, he found one of his most appealing interviewees, a match for the Gloria Counts of *Arsenal for Democracy* or *Arkansas' Black Gold*'s Ruben Dees. (Hill edited more extended pieces on both English and Dees, along with one on Claude Ashmore from *Steamboat's a Comin'*, labeling all three with *[Name] Remembers . . .* titles. We haven't found any record of these ever being broadcast, but all three are preserved in the University of Arkansas's Special Collections archive, where they'll surely prove useful to future researchers.) No film made by Hill so sharply reveals his continuing allegiance to the Statue of Liberty ethos of his country, represented here by his state, as a welcoming haven.

Send your huddled masses. "Build the wall!" was never his chant.

Additional Resources

Maher, Daniel. "Indochinese Resettlement Program." In *Encyclopedia of Arkansas.* Central Arkansas Library System, 2006–. Article last modified December 20, 2017. https://encyclopediaofarkansas.net/entries /indochinese-resettlement-program-5562/.

Malpezzi, Frances M. "Italians." In *Encyclopedia of Arkansas.* Central Arkansas Library System, 2006–. Article last modified May 25, 2017. https://encyclopediaofarkansas .net/entries/italians-2732/.

Schede, Simone. "'Gone but Not Forgotten'—but Almost: The German Heritage of Arkansas." *Amerikastudien/ American Studies* 44, no. 4 (1999): 477–96.

Wiggins, Melanie Spears. "Escape to America: Evacuees from Indochina Arrive in Fort Smith, 1975–1979." *Journal of the Fort Smith Historical Society* 31 (April 2007): 14–29.

Dollar a Day
and All You Can Eat

YEAR OF RELEASE: 2003.

SOURCE: Betacam SP cassette, broadcast tape, aired April/May 2003, box 7, Jack Hill Papers, UA Special Collections.

CAMERAS: Dale Carpenter, Leonard Chamblee.

TITLE: Michael Murphy. Announcer: Rusty Black. Postproduction: Light Productions.

SPONSORS: Butler Center for Arkansas Studies, Electric Cooperatives of Arkansas, Arkansas State Parks, Walmart.

INTERVIEWS: Wendell Barbaree, "Peanut" Daniel, David Davies, Herman Edgin, Louise Fletcher, W. R. Heagler, L. V. Jones, Kelley Kramer, Pauline Kramer, Addie Lee Lister, Polly McKenzie, Hubert Nicholas, Judy Prince, Loyd Stout, Orville Taylor, Ray Willkie.

Dollar a Day and All You Can Eat celebrates the work of Great Depression–era Civilian Conservation Corps (CCC) camps in constructing five state parks in widely separated regions of Arkansas. Devil's Den in the northwest (Washington County), Crowley's Ridge in the northeast (Greene County), Mount Nebo and Petit Jean in the state's center (Yell County), and Lake Catherine farther south (Hot Spring County) are themselves far-flung locations, but approximately seventy thousand Arkansas boys, most of them teenagers, came from every corner of the state, often

Overlook shelter constructed by the CCC in 1934, Devil's Den State Park, Winslow, Arkansas. *Photograph by Sabine Schmidt.*

dropping out of high school to earn thirty dollars a month (and send all but five dollars of it home to dirt-poor families). Poor in heavy machinery but rich in manpower, CCC teams built roads and cut trails with axes and kaiser blades and used chisels and hammers and saws to construct beautiful, remarkably durable stone and timber pavilions and cabins. Many still stand today.

Once again Hill's interviews produce positive retrospective views—men proud of what they made and what their experiences made of them. There was romance, too, for a lucky few—the interview with Kelley and Pauline Kramer is one of the film's highlights. Her father was hopping mad when his seventeen-year-old daughter announced her marriage to a CCC boy at Devil's Den but was much mollified when the camp commander assured him Kelley Kramer was the best man in the whole company. (Not all CCC companies were youngsters—the camps at Mount Nebo and Petit Jean were staffed by World War I veterans.)

Dollar a Day and All You Can Eat features no academic expert—the former workers speak eloquently for themselves. Surely no film Hill made required more shooting locations or more travel for interviews, but it's also true that his own pleasure in the work comes through with unusual clarity. He must have known he'd found a compelling topic and had confidence in his ability to do it justice.

Additional Resources

Laster, Patricia Paulus. "Civilian Conservation Corps (CCC)." In *Encyclopedia of Arkansas*. Central Arkansas Library System, 2006–. Article last modified October 16, 2020. https://encyclopediaofarkansas.net/entries/civilian -conservation-corps-2396/.

Ogilvie, Craig. "Arkansas State Parks: The Legacy of the CCC." Arkansas: The Natural State. Arkansas Department of Parks & Tourism. Published December 26, 2001. https://www.arkansas.com /arkansas-state-parks-legacy-ccc.

A Place Called Home

YEAR OF RELEASE: 2004.

SOURCE: Betacam SP cassette, broadcast tape, aired June 6, 2004, on KHBS, box 7, Jack Hill Papers, UA Special Collections.

CAMERA: Leonard Chamblee.

TITLE: Michael Murphy. Announcer: Rusty Black. Postproduction: Light Productions.

SPONSORS: Arkansas Farm Bureau, Arkansas Humanities Council, Arkansas State University, Craighead Electric Cooperative Corporation, Department of Arkansas Heritage, Lawrence County Chamber of Commerce, Riceland Foods, Walmart.

INTERVIEWS: Tom Baker, Bill Ed Doyle, Weldon Elliott, Bobby Joe Goodwin, Alene Grissom, Delois Jones, Stan Jones, Willene Kirkland, Viola Meadows, Del Pope, Lucille Robbins, Ralph Steele, Wanda Steele, Joe Ward, Robin Whaley, Evelyn Whitmire, Fred Williams.

The Clover Bend community, established in 1937 under the direction of the Farm Security Administration, was one of sixteen New Deal resettlement programs in Arkansas aimed at improving the conditions of life for rural families ravaged by the Great Depression. *A Place Called Home*, opening at a reunion of proud residents and their descendants, showcases Hill at his most affirmative—again and again he listens appreciatively to now elderly people who were children when their lives were changed abruptly for the better by the good fortune of their selection for the project. Families moved for the first time into new homes (many noted with pleased surprise that those homes were *painted*) with the opportunity to own the land they worked. For their children, Clover Bend's high school brought spectacularly increased educational opportunities—most arrived from communities where opportunities for schooling ended at eighth grade.

Hill was once again fortunate in his interviewees —he was always careful of the balance between first-person accounts and the voices of outside authorities, but in Clover Bend he relies almost entirely on the former, and one after another they come through with vivid, memorable narratives with gratitude at their center. Viola Meadows gets top billing—Hill uses her interviews in both his opening and closing section (she chokes up a little in the latter, overcome by the recollection of the larger life opened by her family's move to Clover Bend)—but two or three other interviews are equally effective.

A Place Called Home flirts with the danger of an overstated and unqualified boosterism (not one speaker utters a syllable of complaint), but Hill steps back just a bit at several points. Wonderful as the opportunities were, they were not distributed equably —Hill's narrative points out that Arkansas resettlement programs were segregated by race, with only two of the state's sixteen programs made available to African American applicants. At the close, he describes the programs as among the nation's most ambitious attempts to address rural poverty, adding that later commentary has at times judged them as failures. Bird's-eye, demographic-scale assessments might plausibly reach such conclusions, but *A Place Called Home* offers a ground-level, family-scale perspective, and its overall assessment is emphatically positive.

Additional Resources

Holley, Donald. *Uncle Sam's Farmers: The New Deal Communities in the Lower Mississippi Valley*. Urbana: University of Illinois Press, 1975.

Norman, Bill. "Clover Bend Historic District." In *Encyclopedia of Arkansas*. Central Arkansas Library System, 2006–. Article last modified April 28, 2010. https://encyclopediaofarkansas.net/entries/clover-bend-historic-district-1264/.

Doing What Was Right

YEAR OF RELEASE: 2004.

SOURCE: Betacam SP cassette, broadcast tape, aired November 14, 2004, on KATV, box 42, Jack Hill Papers, UA Special Collections.

CAMERAS: Leonard Chamblee, Dale Carpenter.

TITLE: Michael Murphy. Announcer: Rusty Black. Postproduction: Light Productions.

SPONSORS: Arkansas Department of Parks and Tourism, Arkansas Hospital Association, Arkansas Humanities Council, Century Tel, Department of Arkansas Heritage, Tyson Foods, Walmart.

INTERVIEWS: Sylvia Bell, Betty Bumpers, Dale Bumpers, Tom Dillard, Barbara Dotson, Joe Ferguson, Marion Ferguson, Leroy Jones, Roy Reed, Robin Renfrow, Dale Rice, Archie Shaffer, Maggie Shaffer, LeRoy Williams, Victoria Williams, Alice Wood.

Hill followed up the work on the Clover Bend settlement by turning his attention to the quiet and little-noticed desegregation of the public schools in the Franklin County town of Charleston in 1954, three years prior to the tumultuous events in Little Rock that drew national and international coverage. Dale Bumpers makes an effective lead narrator, but the real stars of the film are his fellow Charleston residents, especially Sylvia Bell, Barbara Dotson, and Joe Ferguson, who appear in great number and at substantial length with their vivid accounts. What first-grader Ruby Bridges, teacher Barbara Henry, and US Marshal Charles Burks accomplished in New Orleans, these folks achieved in Arkansas, with Hill appearing fifty years later as their Norman Rockwell. Their stories are unvarnished—N-word usages are frequent, and injuries done to children linger as visible and audible scars.

Hill's dogged industry here turns up good fortune in at least one parallel that could not have been anticipated. In the final third of the film, Joe Ferguson, who graduated in 1961 in the Charleston high school's first integrated class, looks back over two decades of successful work in aircraft maintenance for FedEx and credits his chemistry and physics classes as giving him confidence that "I can do this." Not three minutes later, Bumpers signs off with a strikingly similar story, crediting his election to the school board in 1958 over a segregationist candidate as giving him an analogous confidence. "Maybe I can convince the people of the state," he thought. Ferguson could, Bumpers did, and Barbara Dotson's niece got it right when she praised her aunt for making access to education possible for her descendants. The result is one of Hill's best films, a quiet story of persistence against bigotry by unheralded people who here receive modest recognition on the fiftieth anniversary of their heroism.

Additional Resources

Erwin, Mary Belle. "Desegregation of Charleston Schools." In *Encyclopedia of Arkansas*. Central Arkansas Library System, 2006–. Article last modified June 24, 2011. https://encyclopediaofarkansas.net/entries/desegregation-of-charleston-schools-730/.

Kirk, John A. "Not Quite Black and White: School Desegregation in Arkansas, 1954–1956." *Arkansas Historical Quarterly* 70, no. 3 (Autumn 2011): 225–57.

Wings of Honor

YEAR OF RELEASE: 2005.

SOURCE: Betacam SP cassette, broadcast tape, aired on AETN, box 34, Jack Hill Papers, UA Special Collections.

CAMERAS: Leonard Chamblee, Steve Childress.

MAPS AND TITLE: Michael Murphy. Announcer: Rusty Black. Postproduction: Light Productions.

SPONSORS: Arkansas Department of Parks and Tourism, Arkansas Humanities Council, Cavenaugh Auto Group, Department of Arkansas Heritage, Williams Baptist College, Walmart.

INTERVIEWS: Regina Bachmann, Jewell Barnett, Robert Bearden, Betty Born, James Brackett, Mary Frances Brackett, Jean Bradfield, O. J. Butts, Buell Crider, Mike Dunn, Dan Ellison, Andy Fair, Lucille Fair, Woodrow Goff, Pat Hicks, Harold Johnson, Wade Jones, Willene Kirkland, Charles Ledbetter, Elroy Lewis, Kelley Presswood, Stanley Rames, Charles Reed, Julian Roadman, Jimmy Snapp, Ed Stallings, Bill Taylor, Billy D. Thornton, Dorothy Willmuth.

If Hill the military history buff found his most favored topic in the American Civil War, films like *Wings of Honor* would join the later *Arsenal for Democracy* and *Faces like Ours* to establish World War II as a clear runner-up. A richly textured documentary mixing thirty interviews (an unusually large number even for Hill) with archival photos, maps, and news clips, *Wings of Honor* chronicles the story of the Walnut Ridge Army Flying School, built in a great hurry in 1942 on just over three thousand Lawrence County acres between Walnut Ridge and Pocahontas to train bomber and fighter plane pilots for wartime service. The hurry brought both benefits and costs—construction and service jobs provided a major economic boost to a region struggling to its feet in the aftermath of the Great Depression, but round-the-clock training schedules with overworked instructors teaching novice pilots resulted in frequent crashes. More than forty cadets and instructors died, but in its roughly two years of operation (October 1942 through June 1944), Walnut Ridge sent nearly five thousand graduates to serve on European and Pacific fronts.

Some died there too, and *Wings of Honor*'s extended closing segment honors Leslie Hood, shot down over Germany on his fiftieth combat mission. Sixty years later Hill interviewed Jean Bradfield, the young Arkansas woman who after the briefest of courtships waited for Hood's letters, first from stateside training fields and then from widely scattered wartime postings. The final letters came from Hood's parents, with the worst of news. Hill devotes great attention to this episode—a fourth of the film's running time. It's a moving story, eloquently told, but beyond this, in this first of his World War II histories, there's a sense of personal tie. Hood died in Germany, in the war Hill's father fought in while his Arkansas mother waited and worried. Hill the citizen and veteran is doing his duty, at attention, offering his filmmaker's salute.

Additional Resources

Hackworth, Bill. "History of the Walnut Ridge Army
 Airfield." *Lawrence County Historical Quarterly* 8, no. 4
 (Fall 1985): 20–24.

Johnson, Harold. "Walnut Ridge Army Flying School." In
 Encyclopedia of Arkansas. Central Arkansas Library
 System, 2006–. Article last modified May 29, 2019.
 https://encyclopediaofarkansas.net/entries/walnut
 -ridge-army-flying-school-2820/.

Wings of Honor Museum. "Expansion of the Army Air
 Forces." Wings of Honor. Accessed October 22, 2021.
 https://www.wingsofhonor.org/expansion-of-army
 -air-forces.html.

New Schools for Arkansas

YEAR OF RELEASE: 2006.

SOURCE: Betacam SP cassette, broadcast tape, aired January 30 and February 18, 2006, on KAIT, box 34, Jack Hill Papers, UA Special Collections.

CAMERAS: Dale Carpenter, Leonard Chamblee, Bob Sandefur.

TITLE: Michael Murphy. Announcer: Rusty Black. Editor: Anthony May. Postproduction: Light Productions.

SPONSORS: Arkansas Blue Cross and Blue Shield, Arkansas Department of Higher Education, Arkansas Department of Parks and Tourism, Arkansas Historic Preservation Program, Arkansas State University, Arkansas Student Loan Authority, Department of Arkansas Heritage.

INTERVIEWS: Ernest Alexander, Nora Briggs, Bertha Creath, Labon Davenport, Charline Davis, Joe Ferguson, Wilber Gaines, Lucille Hankton, Joe Harris, Rebecca Jackson, Lula Jones, Juanita Leverett, Ethel Lucas, J. W. Mason, Kirby Massey, Anetha Parnell, Curtis Pointer, Calvin Smith, Erma Stanley, Bap Sumpter, Samuel Whiting, Harry Whitted, Ralph Wilcox, Rosie Willis, Willie Woodard.

The "new schools" of Hill's title were known in their heyday as Rosenwald Schools, erected primarily for African American students and named in honor of Julius Rosenwald, the wealthy Illinois philanthropist who sponsored the construction of some five thousand of them across the South, mostly in the 1920s.

Nearly four hundred were built in Arkansas, and when Hill took up the subject in 2005, he was just in time to record the memories of students from the late 1930s through the 1950s. From delta towns like Osceola in Mississippi County and Turkey Scratch in Phillips County to Free Hope in Columbia County on the Louisiana border and Little Rock's Dunbar Magnet Middle School, Hill interviewed proud graduates grateful for the life-changing opportunities offered by their newly built schools. The scores of Rosenwald Schools must have reminded the filmmaker of his earlier chronicling of the Fargo Agricultural School—more reunions closed by singings of the school song; similar memories of stern, dedicated teachers mixed in with championship football and basketball teams.

New Schools for Arkansas is one of Hill's warmest efforts, with little of the conspicuous omissions that give a tinge of booster whitewash to *Faces like Ours*. Where *Work Will Win* cited (and photographed) the governor's letter of introduction stressing the "proper relationship of the races," *New Schools for Arkansas* cites the then-current "separate but equal" segregationist educational model only to observe that, separate as they certainly were, "they were not equal." Hill obviously loved such stories of opportunities energetically and gratefully received, from the story of the farm families who won the lottery that got them into the New Deal Clover Bend settlement to that of the women who seized the opportunities offered by wartime employment at the Arkansas Ordnance Plant. If in addition the stories were somehow tied to educational advancement, so much the better.

Additional Resources

Wilcox, Ralph S. "Arkansas Listings in the National Register of Historic Places: Rosenwald Schools." *Arkansas Historical Quarterly* 78, no. 1 (Spring 2019): 84–93.

Wilcox, Ralph S. "Rosenwald Schools." In *Encyclopedia of Arkansas*. Central Arkansas Library System, 2006–. Article last modified March 8, 2021. https://encyclopediaofarkansas.net/entries/rosenwald-schools-2371/.

Arsenal for Democracy

YEAR OF RELEASE: 2006.

SOURCE: Betacam SP cassette, broadcast tape, aired May 29 and June 17, 2006, on KAIT, box 42, Jack Hill Papers, UA Special Collections.

CAMERAS: Leonard Chamblee, Bob Sandefur, Amy Sandefur.

TITLE: Michael Murphy. Announcer: Rusty Black. Postproduction: Light Productions.

SPONSORS: Arkansas Hospital Association, Arkansas Department of Parks and Tourism, Arkansas Humanities Council, Department of Arkansas Heritage, Jacksonville Advertising and Promotion Commission, Walmart.

INTERVIEWS: Gloria Counts, Delphia Culpepper, Wilbur Gentry, Odes Goodsell, Dorothy Gregory, Opal Hays, Fae Jones, Mary Frances Liles, Frank McClure, Trula McGarity, Minnie Moon, Matthew Patnaude, Evelyn Ringgold, C. Calvin Smith, Mildred Whitaker.

Hill's lifelong interest in military history found one of its most compelling subjects in the story of the Arkansas Ordnance Plant (AOP) in Jacksonville. The military importance of the plant is obvious— 88 percent of the bomb fuses and detonators used by American troops in World War II were produced at AOP—but Hill pays greater attention to the plant's social and economic impact. The construction of the AOP turned Jacksonville from a village of four hundred in 1941 to a town of forty thousand a year later. The plant alone was huge, spread out over seven thousand acres and employing over fourteen thousand people, three-fourths of them women and approximately 20 percent African Americans. Wages were unprecedently high by local standards—three or four times the going local rate. A two-hundred-unit trailer park was established, and prefabricated homes and duplexes for five hundred families were quickly erected in a newly established Sunny Side housing project. The completed plant ran twelve production lines on a nonstop three-shift schedule every day but Christmas.

Not much of all this is left, though the Jacksonville Museum of Military History currently displays an AOP guardhouse that must be one of the smallest structures on the National Register of Historic Places (one production line nearby has also been repurposed as a series of retail outlets).

Arkansas State University history professor Calvin Smith serves effectively as the film's central scholarly authority, but *Arsenal for Democracy* features once again Hill's signature cohort of ground-level participants in the story, who recall their youthful times on AOP assembly lines (several lied about their ages to get hired) with justified pride. They liked the money too—for many it was a first paying job, and for virtually all it was a chance to triple and quadruple their wage rate.

One interview in particular offers both a highlight of the film and a glimpse into Hill's tenacity as a researcher. Of the fifteen on-camera interviews that made it into the film, ten are with women who worked in the plant. One of these emerged as the engaging narrator of an unusually vivid story. Gloria Counts used her lunch breaks at AOP, where she had

Arkansas Ordnance Plant guardhouse, Jacksonville Museum of Military History, Jacksonville, Arkansas. *Photograph by Sabine Schmidt.*

access to a typewriter, to correspond with service-men she either knew from high school or had met at United Service Organization (USO) dances. Over time she received and answered hundreds of letters. She saved them all. As he worked, Hill at some point learned of her collection, recognized its appeal, and incorporated it into a featured spot in his film. It's a lovely segment, somehow capturing the heart of a terrifying yet thrilling time when a world at war suddenly opened social and occupational doors for a cohort of central Arkansas young women.

Additional Resources

Basinger, Phillip G. "A History of the Jacksonville Ordnance Plant." *Pulaski County Historical Review* 24, no. 3 (September 1976): 47–55.

Kent, Carolyn Yancey. "Last Hired: African American Hiring in North Pulaski County's Citadel for Defense." *Pulaski County Historical Quarterly* 62, no. 3 (Fall 2014): 77–84.

Kent, Carolyn Yancey. "World War II Ordnance Plants." In *Encyclopedia of Arkansas*. Central Arkansas Library System, 2006–. Article last modified August 25, 2020. https://encyclopediaofarkansas.net/entries/world-war -ii-ordnance-plants-373/.

Smith, C. Calvin. *War and Wartime Changes: The Transformation of Arkansas, 1940–1945*. Fayetteville, AR: University of Arkansas Press, 1986.

Currents of History

YEAR OF RELEASE: 2006.

SOURCE: Betacam SP cassette, broadcast tape, aired on KATV, box 44, Jack Hill Papers, UA Special Collections.

CAMERAS: Leonard Chamblee, Steve Childress, Bob Sandefur.

TITLE AND MAP: Michael Murphy. Announcer: Rusty Black. Production Assistants: Cody Bennett, James Groves. Postproduction: Light Productions.

SPONSORS: Arkansas Farm Bureau, Arkansas' Ozark Gateway Region, Arkansas State Parks, Arkansas State University, Butler Center for Arkansas Studies, Days Inn, Pocahontas Sesquicentennial, Walmart.

INTERVIEWS: Morris Arnold, Justin Dorsey, Michael Dougan, Travis Eddleman, Christina French, Bennie Jarrett, Luttie Mae Johnson, David Looney, Cindy Robinett, Harmon Seawel, Elsie Young.

Currents of History is right up there with *Work Will Win* in the race for most opaque title of a Jack Hill film. Both are catchy and ultimately make sense—"Work Will Win" was the motto of the Fargo Agricultural School that brought spectacularly expanded educational opportunities to young African American Arkansans in the 1920s and '30s, and it turns out that Northeast Arkansas's Randolph County is home to five significant rivers—but neither title offers the slightest hint of the film's central subject. That subject here is Randolph County itself as home to a great number of Arkansas "firsts"—Davidsonville didn't last long as a town (it was nearly abandoned before 1830), but in the previous decade, it boasted the then territory's first courthouse, a splendid brick structure erected in Arkansas's oldest planned town. Two of the state's oldest still-standing homes—the Looney-French House and the Rice-Upshaw House—are featured in the film.

Currents of History concentrates attention on the families who settled the area—they came early and stayed, and Hill seeks out their descendants for accounts of their enduring attachment. One of these, Bennie Jarrett, proudly introduces his granddaughter as a seventh-generation resident. Many of these pioneers came with slaves, who also stayed—over two hundred people were held in bondage in Randolph County when the Civil War broke out. Hill's interviews with their descendants add a chilling depth to the portrait. Elsie Young, for example, recalls on camera the fate of a grandmother's brother: "They put him up on a stump and bidded him off, and the highest bidder bought him."

Additional Resources

Cande, Kathleen H. "Rediscovering Davidsonville, Arkansas's First County Seat Town, 1815–1830" *Arkansas Historical Quarterly* 67, no. 4 (Winter 2008): 342–58.

Gould, Joan L. "Rice-Upshaw House." In *Encyclopedia of Arkansas*. Central Arkansas Library System, 2006–. Article last modified March 22, 2017. https://encyclopediaofarkansas.net/entries/rice-upshaw-house-7050/.

Gould, Joan L. "William Looney Tavern." In *Encyclopedia*

of Arkansas. Central Arkansas Library System, 2006–. Article last modified March 22, 2017. https://encyclo pediaofarkansas.net/entries/william-looney-tavern -7051/.

Jones, Kelly Houston. "'A Rough, Saucy Set of Hands to Manage': Slave Resistance in Arkansas." *Arkansas Historical Quarterly* 71, no. 1 (Spring 2012): 1–21.

Faces like Ours

YEAR OF RELEASE: 2009.

SOURCE: DVCPRO cassette, broadcast tape, aired on AETN, box 40, Jack Hill Papers, UA Special Collections.

CAMERAS: Steve Childress, Dale Carpenter, Leonard Chamblee.

AUDIO ENGINEERS: James Groves, Thomas Rogers. Title and Map: Michael Murphy. Announcer: Rusty Black. Video Editing: Thomas Rogers.

SPONSORS: Arkansas Historic Preservation Program, Delta Cultural Center, Department of Arkansas Heritage.

INTERVIEWS: Jerry Caldwell, Bernice Chapin, Erika Cohen, Billy Joe Emerson, Mary Hall, William Harrison, Rosemary Hooks, Bettye Kellum, Lorraine Kerksieck, O. B. Neal, Michael Pomeroy, Steve Rucker, William Shea, Tom Sponer.

Faces like Ours takes its title from a German World War II POW's memoir describing the faces of his American captors. The film tells the story of the nearly twenty-five thousand Italian and German POWs brought to four main camps and many satellite work stations in Arkansas beginning in 1943. The focus throughout is on their interactions not with their military custodians but with civilians who encountered them in work assignments or other circumstances. The result is a determinedly feel-good film—southern hospitality trumps wartime hostility.

The stories themselves are heartwarming: grateful Italian prisoners at Camp Monticello present an oil portrait to the doctor who made repeated prison house calls on their behalf; a farmer whose crops are saved by prison labor crews serves them cold beers before trucks arrive to return them to their barracks. There's also an amazing saga of a persistent, ultimately successful effort by a young man to return to its POW author a prison diary he found by the side of a road near Jonesboro.

But all the warmth feels a bit off-key, especially when one considers how much has been carefully omitted. What of the Japanese Americans, for example, well over half of them US citizens, who were also imprisoned in Arkansas camps ("interned" is the euphemism, but there were guard towers manned by armed soldiers)? Even more strikingly absent are the African American Arkansans, every one of them citizens at least nominally free, who lived and worked at the camps but could only envy the incomparably higher standard of food and shelter provided for prisoners and internees inside the wires. What of all these folks, the ones with faces not so much like "ours"?

Faces like Ours is one of Hill's last films. His methods are second nature by this time—the down-to-earth interviews, the smooth transitions from archival film and news clips to present-day settings. Perhaps it's the topic, or more precisely the too-obvious cherry picking of the topic, that unsettles. One misses the occasional analytic step back that saved *A Place Called Home* from a similar boosterism.

Additional Resources

Bowman, Michael. "World War II Prisoner of War Camps in Arkansas." In *Encyclopedia of Arkansas*. Central Arkansas Library System, 2006–. Article last modified December 30, 2020. https://encyclopediaofarkansas .net/entries/world-war-ii-prisoner-of-war-camps-2398/

Shea, William L., and Edwin Pelz. "The German Prisoner of War in the South: The Memoir of Edwin Pelz." *Arkansas Historical Quarterly* 44, no. 1 (Spring 1985): 42–55.

THE
ARKANSAS
SERIES

War in the '60s

YEAR OF RELEASE: 2014.

SOURCE: Video, first aired May 15, 2014, on AETN, https://www.myarkansaspbs.org/programs/warinthe60s.

CAMERA: uncredited.

TITLE: uncredited. Announcer: uncredited. Postproduction: uncredited.

SPONSOR: Arkansas Historic Preservation Program.

Interviews: Tarry Beasley, Robert Bell, Don Bunch, Kevin Butler, Thomas Cartwright, Mark Christ, Tom DeBlack, Herb Jackson, Townsend Moseley, Bobby Roberts, William Shea, Charlie Speaerman, Jeannie Wayne.

War in the '60s was left unfinished at Hill's death in 2012. Edited to completion by longtime cameraman Dale Carpenter, it marks a return to the early years of TeleVision for Arkansas, to 1992's *War Comes to Arkansas*, 1993's *War in the Delta*, and 1997's *War on the Frontier*, in an attempt to cover in a single film the whole span of the Civil War as it was experienced in Arkansas (and by Arkansas soldiers on more distant battlefields).

Carpenter remembers the film's making:

> When Jack was diagnosed with cancer, I heard he was at Mercy Hospital in Rogers. The first time I went to visit him I didn't know what to expect, and I remember wondering what would be some

good things we could talk about that Jack would enjoy. I knew he was working on a film about the Civil War in Arkansas, so the first question I asked was "How's the film going?" He talked for an hour about the film. He had the entire script memorized, and he recited it to me, along with visual descriptions. He had just begun editing the film when he got sick. After Jack died, I was able to get a copy of the script and all the videotapes he was using from the production company in Little Rock where he was editing. Everything was there, including his obligatory opening stand-up and close and all of his narration. I knew the best thing I could do to honor Jack would be to finish his film. Editing *War in the '60s* brought back a flood of memories about long days with Jack in places all over the state. It made me realize how lucky I was that he'd asked me to help him tell all those wonderful stories about Arkansas.

Additional Resources

Bailey, Anne, and Daniel E. Sutherland, eds. *Civil War Arkansas: Beyond Battles and Leaders*. Fayetteville, AR: University of Arkansas Press, 2000.

Christ, Mark K., and Patrick G. Williams, eds. *I Do Wish This Cruel War Was Over: First-Person Accounts of Civil War Arkansas from the 'Arkansas Historical Quarterly.'* Fayetteville, AR: University of Arkansas Press, 2014.

BONUS TRACKS

The Attack

YEAR OF RELEASE: 1985.

SOURCE: U-matic cassette, broadcast tape, aired June 8, 1985, on KAIT, box 11, Jack Hill Papers, UA Special Collections.

CAMERA: Manochehr Nourizadeh.

SPONSOR: KAIT-TV.

This short unedited clip is by almost a decade the earliest bit of film included in our selection, as well as the only one not produced by Hill as an independent filmmaker. Lacking a title card, captioning, or credits, it shows Hill, still working for KAIT, standing in the dark with a cameraman, microphone in hand, on a roadside near a rural house in St. Francis County. He's there pursuing KAIT's ongoing investigation of illegal gambling activities suspected of being at least countenanced if not actively sponsored by Sheriff Coolidge Conlee. As the clip opens, Hill is approached by a man later identified as Deputy

Sheriff Calvin Adams, who refuses to identify himself but describes the house as the residence of Delton Cummings and the event in progress as a birthday party. Adams then suddenly seizes Hill's microphone and attacks the newsman, swinging it at him by its cord. Hill retreats, and Adams at first pursues but then turns toward the cameraman, who has filmed the entire episode. There are brief shots of the spotlighted roadway and the rear fender of Hill's car (but no audio) before the screen goes blank.

For all its brevity, the clip captures the beginning of a terrifying interlude for Hill. His camera operator, an Arkansas State University graduate student named Manochehr Nourizadeh, managed to escape in the car, stop at a nearby farmhouse, and summon help by calling the KAIT offices. But Hill spent several hours hiding in the woods, initially afraid to reveal himself even when he heard voices calling his name, for fear of being apprehended by Conlee's confederates instead of rescued by the state police. He'd been in Cold War Berlin and Iron Curtain Moscow, but this was *Deliverance* and *Easy Rider* country, and he was terrified.

We include this raw fragment for its vivid glimpse of Hill's courage and commitment to his work. In the clip's opening moments, he steps right up to the bellicose Adams, sticks a microphone in his face, tells him he's on camera, and starts popping questions. In its final seconds, Hill is last seen chasing his assailant, rushing to the aid of the cameraman now under assault.

Less than two months later he'd be fired for refusal to "redirect his general journalistic concepts."

Additional Resources

Meins, Jan. "Still No Charges in Attack on 2 Newsmen." *Arkansas Democrat*, April 20, 1986.

Reel, Guy. *Unequal Justice: Wayne Dumond, Bill Clinton, and the Politics of Rape in Arkansas.* Buffalo: Prometheus Books, 1993.

"The Law and Sheriff Conlee," transcript of *20/20*, episode 902, January 13, 1989. Jack Hill papers. University of Arkansas Special Collections Division, box 78.

Festivals and World Championships (Excerpt)

YEAR OF RELEASE: 1998.

SOURCE: Betacam SP cassette, MC 1355, series 2, box 3T, tape 38, Jack Hill Papers, UA Special Collections.

CAMERAS: Dale Carpenter, David Settlemoir.

TITLE: Michael Murphy. Announcer: Rusty Black. Production Coordinator: Joanne Elliott. Postproduction: Light Productions.

SPONSORS: Arkansas Department of Parks and Tourism, Arkansas Festival Association, Arkansas Public Schools, Heifer Project International, Langley Oil Company, Smackover Chamber of Commerce, United Methodist Church, Walmart.

INTERVIEWS (IN EXCERPTED CLIP): Ernie Emerson, Denise Henderson, Pam Stevens.

The state of Arkansas, Hill asserts in his opening stand-up, is host each year to some twelve hundred festivals, an astonishing total. *Festivals and World Championships*, using footage from several earlier titles—*The Way It Was* and *Arkansas' Black Gold* among them—visits seven such events, offering a rare glimpse of Hill turning his attention to the lighter side of life in Arkansas. Even here, however, there is his usual attention to geographical distribution. First to be featured is the Purple Hull Pea Festival and World Championship Rotary Tiller

Race held in Emerson, a tiny town near the Louisiana border in Columbia County, followed by the since-discontinued Mosquito Cook-Off at Crowley's Ridge State Park, the World Championship Quartz Crystal Dig in Mount Ida, and (oldest and best-known of the lot) the World Championship Duck Calling Contest held in conjunction with the Wings Over the Prairie Festival in Stuttgart.

Each segment has its offbeat appeal—the fanciers of mosquito cuisine win most bizarre competition hands down, and the quartz diggers stand out for their enjoyment of their hot and dirty play—but the just over four minutes devoted near the beginning to the hot-rod tillers must be seen to be fully appreciated. Hill's voice is a prominent presence on the soundtrack, but he stays out of the video in this clip.

Additional Resources

Oddly, there is a conspicuous dearth of published research on tiller racing, but in 2016 *Wall Street Journal* reporter Beckie Strum journeyed to Emerson and produced "Soil and Gas: Two Arkansas Families Battle for World Supremacy in Rototiller Racing," *Wall Street Journal*, July 1, 2016, https://www.wsj.com/articles/soil-and-gas-two-arkansas-families-battle-for-world-supremacy-in-rototiller-racing-1467382759.

Arkansas' Hemingway
(Excerpt)

YEAR OF RELEASE: 2003.

SOURCE: Betacam SP cassette, broadcast tape, aired on AETN, box 52, Jack Hill Papers, UA Special Collections.

CAMERAS: James Groves, Dale Carpenter, Leonard Chamblee.

TITLE: Michael Murphy. Announcer: Rusty Black. Postproduction: Light Productions.

SPONSORS: Arkansas Department of Parks and Tourism, Arkansas State University, Downtown Inn, Hemingway-Pfeiffer Museum and Educational Center, Piggott Chamber of Commerce, Walmart

INTERVIEWS (IN EXCERPTED CLIP): Jack Ballard, Vernell Bradshaw, Camilla Cox, Paul O'Dell, "Frosty" Smith, Denver Stokes.

This two-and-a-half-minute sequence comes near the close of Hill's chronicle of Ernest Hemingway's intermittent residence in Piggott, Arkansas, between 1928 and 1940 as the husband of Pauline Pfeiffer, a daughter of the town's wealthiest family. Hill has joined a group of oldster regulars at Piggott's Hardee's restaurant to hear their recollections of the celebrity author they took for a derelict and treated with unthinking schoolboy abuse. For all its brevity, it catches Hill at his best. As buttoned-up as ever, he's nevertheless clearly enjoying himself. The camerawork is unobtrusively adroit—note the effective close-ups of every speaker at the closely packed table, including Hill in attentive listening mode. Dale Carpenter brings a professional cameraman's perspective to the moment: "James Groves probably shot it. They probably shot the interviews first, then Jack continued to jaw with them while James picked up the extra shots. James had the good sense to use a tripod and limit the camera movement. He made sure to get shots of the guys listening and reacting. And he got the big wide shot that shows the whole group seated."

This scene is a high point in a film with a higher-than-usual helping of filler—several largely irrelevant minutes devoted to a quilt show in the Pfeiffer home stand out as a low point.

Additional Resources

Hawkins, Ruth. *Unbelievable Happiness and Final Sorrow: The Hemingway-Pfeiffer Marriage.* Fayetteville, AR: University of Arkansas Press, 2012.

NOTES

Introduction

1. Roy Ockert, "Hill's Work Added to Understanding State," *Northwest Arkansas Democrat Gazette*, July 23, 2012, https://www.nwaonline.com/news/2012/jul/23/hill146s-work-added-to-understanding-state/; and Steven Watkins, "Jack Hill: The Final Sign-Off for a Local News Legend," *Steve Watkins Media* (blog), July 14, 2012, https://stevenwwatkins.wordpress.com/tag/jack-hill-obituary/. The photograph accompanying the Ockert article is of Ockert, not of Jack Hill.

2. Ezra Pound, *ABC of Reading* (New York: New Directions, 1934), 29, https://www.google.com/books/edition/ABC_of_Reading/mUDyEiVqxpsC?hl=en&gbpv=0.

Chapter 1

1. Rogers High School, "Mountaineer Time," in *The Mountaineer* yearbook (Rogers, AR: 1957).

2. Rogers High School, *The Mountaineer* yearbook (Rogers, AR: 1958).

3. Mack Luffman (childhood friend of Jack Hill), in discussion with the authors, Rogers, AR, October 7, 2018.

4. Jack Hill to his parents and others, newsletter, November 25, 1963, box 15, Jack Hill Papers, University of Arkansas Library Special Collections Division. This is the fourth letter in the sequence. Hill described the set as "newsletters."

5. Jack Hill to his parents and others, August 20, 1964, box 24, Jack Hill Papers. This is the seventh (and final) letter in the sequence.

6. Jack Hill to his parents and others, April 13, 1963, box 15, Jack Hill Papers. This is the second letter in the sequence.

7. Jack Hill to his parents and others, August 19, 1963,

box 15, Jack Hill Papers. This is the third letter in the sequence.

8. Jack Hill to his parents and others, May 28, 1964, box 24, Jack Hill Papers.

9. Hill to his parents and others, May 28, 1964.

10. Hill to his parents and others, May 28, 1964.

11. Jack Hill to his parents and others, March 16, 1964, box 15, Jack Hill Papers. This is the fifth letter in the sequence.

12. Hill to his parents and others, August 20, 1964.

13. Hill to his parents and others, August 19, 1963.

14. Hill to his parents and others, August 20, 1964.

15. Hill to his parents and others, March 16, 1964.

16. Hill to his parents and others, August 20, 1964.

17. Hill to his parents and others, August 20, 1964.

18. Hill to his parents and others, August 20, 1964.

19. Jack Hill to Bill Henry (then news director at station WFLA-TV in Tampa, FL), March 23, 1968, box 53, Jack Hill Papers, University of Arkansas Library Special Collections Division.

20. University of Arkansas, *Razorback* (Fayetteville, AR: 1962), 186, University of Arkansas Library. All of the 1959–62 issues were examined at the University of Arkansas Library.

21. Hill to his parents and others, April 13, 1963.

22. Hill to his parents and others, April 13, 1963.

23. Hill to his parents and others, November 25, 1963.

24. Hill to his parents and others, November 25, 1963.

25. Hill to his parents and others, March 16, 1964.

26. Hill to his parents and others, August 20, 1964.

27. Hill to Henry, March 23, 1968.

28. Jack Edward Hill, "A Survey of Network Television's Coverage of the War in Vietnam" (master's thesis, University of Missouri, 1967), 1, 3, 5.

29. Hill, "Network Television's Coverage," 117–18.

30. Hill, "Network Television's Coverage," 86.

31. Hill, "Network Television's Coverage," 109.

32. Hill, "Network Television's Coverage," 53–54

33. Jack Hill, "Unequal Justice under the Law: And the Arkansas Media's Role in It; An Analytical Memoir on Journalistic Performance" (unpublished manuscript, February 28, 1989), typescript.

34. Hill to Henry, March 23, 1968.

35. Jack Hill to Charles Caton (news director of WSFA-TV), March 28, 1968, box 53, Jack Hill Papers, University of Arkansas Library Special Collections Division.

36. Jack Hill to Dave Mieher (news director of WLBT-WJDX), April 19, 1968, box 53, Jack Hill Papers, University of Arkansas Library Special Collections Division.

37. Robert F. Lewine (president of the National Academy of Television Arts and Sciences) to Dave Mieher, February 10, 1971, box 53, Jack Hill Papers, University of Arkansas Library Special Collections Division.

38. Anne Hill, email message to authors, October 6, 2018.

39. Luffman, discussion.

40. Carroll Fulgham (*Homes like These* cameraman), in discussion with the authors, December 15, 2018.

41. Anne Hill, email message to authors, December 6, 2018.

42. William G. Thomas III, "Television News and the Civil Rights Struggle: The Views in Virginia and Mississippi," *Southern Spaces*, November 2004, https://southern-spaces.org/2004/television-news-and-civil-rights -struggle-views-virginia-and-mississippi/. See especially the section headed "WLBT and Pro-Segregation TV."

43. Fulgham, discussion.

44. Jack Hill, script for December 18, 1969, news broadcast, box 53, Jack Hill Papers, University of Arkansas Library Special Collections Division.

45. Fulgham, discussion; and Anne Hill, email message to authors, December 6, 2018.

46. Memorandum to "Management," "The Problems in the Newsroom," February 5, 1971, box 53, Jack Hill Papers, University of Arkansas Library Special Collections Division. Four names are appended to the document's close, with Dave Mieher marked as receiving the original and Mark Ledbetter, Bob McRaney Jr., and Harland Knight cc'd. McRaney was the station manager.

47. Frank Hains, "On Stage," *Jackson Daily News*, May 31, 1971, 4, box 53, Jack Hill Papers, University of Arkansas Library Special Collections Division.

48. Anne Hill, email message to authors, December 6, 2018.

49. Jack Hill, draft report from Mena airport, September 1973, box 53, Jack Hill Papers, University of Arkansas Special Collections Division.

50. Jack Hill, scripts for Dallas traffic congestion series, box 53, Jack Hill Papers, University of Arkansas Special Collections Division.

51. Dennis Holder, "The Spirit of Tension," *D Magazine*, March 1989, https://www.dmagazine.com/publications/d-magazine/1989/march/the-spirit-of-tension/.

52. Anne Hill, in discussion with the authors, December 21, 2018.

53. Anne Hill, email message to authors, December 6, 2018.

Chapter 2

1. George T. Hernreich, commenting in the *KAIT 25th Anniversary Special*, aired 1988, on KAIT, video, 23:31, https://spark.adobe.com/page/AlS8ZQKtPiy9d/.

2. John Knott, "KAIT Gobbles the Market in NE Arkansas," *Commercial Appeal* (Memphis), April 19, 1981, 16.

3. *KAIT 25th Anniversary Special.*

4. *KAIT 25th Anniversary Special.*

5. Knott, "KAIT Gobbles the Market," 16.

6. Darrel Cunningham (former station manager at KAIT), in discussion with the authors, Ft. Smith, AR, October 23, 2018.

7. Cunningham, discussion.

8. Cunningham, discussion.

9. Ray Scales (former KAIT cameraman) and Becky Allison (former KAIT anchor), in discussion with the authors, Jonesboro, AR, July 14, 2018.

10. Scales and Allison, discussion.

11. "Award," Sun off the Beaten Path, *Jonesboro Sun*, September 2, 1982, box 73, Jack Hill Papers, University of Arkansas Library Special Collections Division.

12. Scales and Allison, discussion.

13. "KAIT Sued," *Blytheville Courier News*, May 31, 1980, 1.

14. Darrel Cunningham, email message to the authors, April 15, 2020.

15. Mike Trimble, "KAIT-TV: Small but Quite Effective," *Arkansas Gazette*, September 23, 1979, 11F.

16. Cunningham, discussion, October 23, 2018.

17. James Polk, "TV Strengths," *IRE Journal*, Fall 1981, 3, box 73, Jack Hill Papers, University of Arkansas Library Special Collections Division.

18. IRE 1981 National Conference Program, box 73, Jack Hill Papers, University of Arkansas Library Special Collections Division.

19. Trimble, "KAIT-TV," 2F.

20. Cunningham, discussion.

21. Knott, "KAIT Gobbles the Market," 16.

22. Cunningham, discussion.

23. Darrel Cunningham, email message to the authors, January 20, 2020.

24. Hillary Rodham, interview by Jack Hill, *In Focus*, KAIT, January 1979, https://www.youtube.com/watch?v= bg_sEZg7-rk&t=5s. All quotations have been transcribed from this broadcast by the authors.

25. Rodham, interview.

26. Anne Hill, in discussion with the authors, Little Rock, September 15, 2016.

27. Scales and Allison, discussion.

28. Scales and Allison, discussion.

29. Scales and Allison, discussion.

30. Cunningham, discussion.

31. Cunningham, discussion.

32. Anne Hill, email message to the authors, July 16, 2019.

33. Ockert, "Hill's Work."

34. Cunningham, discussion.

35. Cunningham, discussion.

36. Roy Ockert Jr., "TV Station Takes Ax to Coverage," *Batesville Daily Guard*, August 1, 1985, 2, box 67, Jack Hill Papers, University of Arkansas Library Special Collections Division.

37. Mark Carnopis, "Reporter Relieved by Indictment of Ex-Sheriff," *Arkansas Democrat*, May 26, 1988, 8B, box 67, Jack Hill Papers, University of Arkansas Library Special Collections Division.

38. Guy Reel, *Unequal Justice: Wayne Dumond, Bill Clinton, and the Politics of Rape in Arkansas* (Buffalo: Prometheus Books, 1993), 56–57, 68–69.

39. Reel, *Unequal Justice*, 214.
40. "Balancing the Scales," *Arkansas Democrat*, June 2, 1988, 6B.
41. Reel, *Unequal Justice*, 170.
42. John Robert Starr to Jack Hill, November 21, 1985, box 69, Jack Hill Papers, University of Arkansas Library Special Collections Division.
43. Thomas Tyrer and Laura Malt, "RTNDA Honors Stations for Investigative Reports," *Electronic Media*, September 24, 1990, S2.
44. Anne Hill, email message to the authors, July 16, 2019.
45. Anne Hill, email message to the authors, August 19, 2019.
46. Hill, "Unequal Justice," 25, 37.
47. *The Encyclopedia of Arkansas*, s.v. "Wayne Eugene DuMond (1949–2005)," by Ernest Dumas, last modified September 8, 2021, https://encyclopediaofarkansas.net/entries/wayne-eugene-dumond-8005/.
48. Nan Snider, "Whatever Happened to Jack Hill," *Northeast Arkansas Town Crier*, November 4, 1987, 1.
49. Snider, "Whatever Happened to Jack Hill," 2.

Chapter 3

1. Anne Hill, email message to the authors, July 16, 2019.
2. Anne Hill, email message to the authors, July 16, 2019.
3. Hill, discussion, September 15, 2016.
4. Hill, discussion, September 15, 2016.
5. Anne Hill, email message to the authors, January 17, 2020.
6. Jack E. Hill, proposal to the Walton Family Charitable Support Foundation, Inc, for "The Arkansas Series of video tapes," April 1, 2003, box 29A, Jack Hill Papers, University of Arkansas Library Special Collections Division.
7. Jack Hill, proposal draft, n.d., ca. 2002, box 29, Jack Hill Papers, University of Arkansas Library Special Collections Division.
8. "Jack Hill Productions on AETN," *AETN Program Guide*, November 1996, box 3, Jack Hill Papers,

University of Arkansas Library Special Collections
Division.

9. Michael Storey, "The TV Column," *Arkansas Democrat-Gazette*, June 5, 2005, 3E.

10. Michael Storey, "The TV Column," *Arkansas Democrat-Gazette*, January 31, 2006.

11. Michael Storey, "The TV Column," *Arkansas Democrat-Gazette*, May 28, 2006.

12. Michael Storey, "The TV Column," *Arkansas Democrat-Gazette*, October 1, 2006, 3E.

13. Michael Storey, "The TV Column," *Arkansas Democrat-Gazette*, April 9, 2009, 2E; and Michael Storey, "The TV Column," *Arkansas Democrat-Gazette*, November 18, 2010, 2E.

14. "Grace F. Hill: Rogers, AR, 1915–2012," *Northwest Arkansas Democrat-Gazette*, May 27, 2012, https://www.nwaonline.com/obituaries/2012/may/27/grace-hill-2012-05-27/.

15. Anne Hill, email message to the authors, April 18, 2020.

16. Dale Carpenter, eulogy for Jack Hill, delivered by Dale Carpenter, July 20, 2012, printed copy in the author's possession.

17. Anne Hill, email message to the authors, December 27, 2020.

18. Charles Portis, *The Dog of the South* (New York: Overlook Press, 1999), 255.

INDEX

English, Alpha, 98, 99, 124, 134
Eureka Springs Chamber of Commerce, 89
Evers, Medgar, 36

F

Fahrenheit 9/11 (documentary film), 83
Fargo Agricultural School (FAS), 85, 103, 109, 110, 120–21, 122, 148, 154
  Fargo Agricultural School Museum, 121
Fargo (Arkansas), 120–22
Farm Security Administration (FSA), 139
Fayetteville (Arkansas), 15, 45, 86, 103
Ferguson, Joe, 97, 98, 124, 142
Ferritor, Dan, 126
Flower Films, 83
Fordyce (Arkansas), 84
Forrest City (Arkansas), 68, 70
Fort Smith (Arkansas), 45, 54, 67, 100, 103, 132, 134
Franklin County (Arkansas), 142
Free Hope (Arkansas), 148
Fulbright, J. William, 59, 76
Fulgham, Carroll, 35, 37–40
Fuller, W. H., 96
Fuller, W. H., Mrs., 96

G

Gabriel Awards Certificate of Merit, 53
Gaines, L. N., 13
The Gene Williams Country Junction Show, 45–46
Georgia-Pacific, 89, 110
Gould (Arkansas), 82
Grace F. Hill Elementary School, 125
Grape Festival (Tontitown, Arkansas), 100, 134
Gray Television, 117
Green, Sylvester, 64, 109
Greene County (Arkansas), 136
Grimes, Bonnie, 106
Groves, James, 169
Guatemala, 54
Gulfport (Mississippi), 34

H

Haag, Marty, 43
Hall, John Wesley, 71, 73

University of Mississippi, 37
University of Missouri, 22, 26–30, 46, 52, 63

V

Van Buren (Arkansas), 126
Village Voice (New York City newspaper), 69

W

Wall Street Journal (New York City newspaper), 167
Walmart, 87, 88, 89, 100, 102, 131
Walnut Ridge (Arkansas), 145
Walnut Ridge Army Flying School, 16, 103, 145, 146
Walton Family Charitable Support Foundation, 88
Walton, Rob, 87, 88
Washington (Arkansas), 116
Washington County (Arkansas), 136
Wasson, Cal, 60
WFAA (Dallas, Texas television station), 41, 43–44, 85
"Whatever Happened to Jack Hill?," 75
White Citizens Council (Mississippi), 36, 39
White River, 95, 129, 130, 133
Wings Over the Prairie Festival, 167
Winslow (Arkansas), 137
Winthrop Rockefeller Foundation, 76
WLBT-WJDX (Jackson, Mississippi, television station),
    33–41, 44
Wood, Terry, 47, 61
World Championship Duck Calling Contest, 167
World Championship Quartz Crystal Dig, 167
WSFA-TV (Montgomery, Alabama, television station), 32

Y

Yekaterinburg (Russia), 101
Yell County (Arkansas), 100, 136
Yohe, Mrs. Carl, 128
Young, Elsie, 155